PRACTIC SOCIAL WORK

Series Editor: Jo Campling

BASW

Editorial Advisory Board:
Robert Adams, Terry Bamford, Charles Barker, Lena Dominelli,
Malcolm Payne, Michael Preston-Shoot, Daphne Statham and
Jane Tunstill

Social work is at an important stage in its development. All professions must be responsive to changing social and economic conditions if they are to meet the needs of those they serve. This series focuses on sound practice and the specific contribution which social workers can make to the well-being of our society in the 1990s.

The British Association of Social Workers has always been conscious of its role in setting guidelines for practice and in seeking to raise professional standards. The conception of the Practical Social Work series arose from a survey of BASW members to discover where they, the practitioners in social work, felt there was the most need for new literature. The response was overwhelming and enthusiastic, and the result is a carefully planned, coherent series of books. The emphasis is firmly on practice, set in a theoretical framework. The books will inform, stimulate and promote discussion, thus adding to the further development of skills and high professional standards. All the authors are practitioners and teachers of social work, representing a wide variety of experience.

JO CAMPLING

Robert Adams *Self-Help, Social Work and Empowerment*

David Anderson *Social Work and Mental Handicap*

Robert Brown, Stanley Bute and Peter Ford *Social Workers at Risk*

Alan Butler and Colin Pritchard *Social Work and Mental Illness*

Roger Clough *Residential Work*

David M. Cooper and David Ball *Social Work and Child Abuse*

Veronica Coulshed *Management in Social Work*

Veronica Couldshed *Social Work Practice: An introduction (2nd edn)*

Paul Daniel and John Wheeler *Social Work and Local Politics*

Peter R. Day *Sociology in Social Work Practice*

Lena Dominelli *Anti-Racist Social Work:A Challenge for White Practitioners and Educators*

Celia Doyle *Working with Abused Children*

Geoff Fimister *Welfare Rights Work in Social Services*

Kathy Ford and Alan Jones *Student Supervision*

Alison Froggatt *Family Work with Elderly People*

Danya Glaser and Stephen Frost *Child Sexual Abuse*

Gill Gorell Barnes *Working with Families* ✓

Jalna Hanmer and Daphne Statham *Women and Social Work:Towards a Woman-Centred Practice*

Tony Jeffs and Mark Smith *Youth Work* ✓

Michael Kerfoot and Alan Butler *Problems of Childhood and Adolescence* ✓

Mary Marshall *Social Work with Old People (2nd edn)*

Paula Nicolson and Rowan Bayne *Applied Psychology for Social Workers (2nd edn)*

Kieran O'Hagan *Crisis Intervention in Social Services*

Michael Oliver *Social Work with Disabled People* ✓

Lisa Parkinson *Separation, Divorce and Families* ✓

Malcolm Payne *Social Care in the Community*

Malcolm Payne *Working in Teams*

John Pitts *Working with Young Offenders* ✓

Michael Preston-Shoot *Effective Groupwork*

Carole R. Smith *Adoption and Fostering: Why and How*

Carole R. Smith *Social Work with the Dying and Bereaved*

Carole R. Smith, Marty T. Lane and Terry Walshe *Child Care and the Courts* ✓

Alan Twelvetrees *Community Work (2nd edn)*

Hilary Walker and Bill Beaumount (eds) *Working with Offenders*

FORTHCOMING TITLES

Jim Barber *Social Work Practice*

Lynne Berry, Cressy Cannan and Karen Lyons *Social Work in Europe*

Suzy Braye and Michael Preston-Shoot *Practising Social Work Law*

Suzy Croft and Peter Beresford *Involving the Consumer*

Angela Everitt, Pauline Hardiker, Jane Littlewood and Audrey Millender *Applied Research for Better Practice*

Michael Freeman *The Children's Act 1989*

Cordelia Grimwood and Ruth Poppleston *Women, Management and Care*

David Hebblewhite and Tom Leckie *Social Work with Addictions*

Paul Henderson and David Francis *Working with Rural Communities*

Rosemary Jefferson and Mike Shooter *Preparing for Practice*

Jeremy Kearney and Dave Evans *A Systems Approach to Social Work*

Joyce Lishman *Communication and Social Work*

Carole Lupton (ed) *Working with Violence*

Graham McBeath and Stephen Webb *The Politics of Social Work*

Steven Shardlow and Mark Doel *Practice: Learning and Teaching*

Gill Stewart and John Stewart *Social Work and Housing*

Community Work

Second Edition

Alan Twelvetrees

First published 1982 by
THE MACMILLAN PRESS LTD
Houndmills, Basingstoke, Hampshire RG21 2XS
and London
Companies and representatives
throughout the world

ISBN 0–333–49505–5 (hardcover)
ISBN 0–333–49506–3 (paperback)

A catalogue record for this book is available
from the British Library

Printed in Hong Kong

Reprinted 1985, 1986, 1987, 1988
Second edition 1991
Reprinted 1992

Series Standing Order
If you would like to receive future titles in this series as they are published, you can make use of our standing order facility. To place a standing order please contact your bookseller or, in case of difficulty, write to us at the address below with your name and address and the name of the series. Please state with which title you wish to begin your standing order. (If you live outside the United Kingdom we may not have the rights for your area, in which case we will forward your order to the publisher concerned.)

Customer Services Department, Macmillan Distribution Ltd, Houndmills, Basingstoke, Hampshire RG21 2XS, England.

Contents

Foreword

When the new model of a particular type of car comes out it may look very much the same as the previous one. But it can be quite different under the bonnet.

It's a bit like that with this book. I wrote the earlier edition in the 1980s and based nearly all of what I wrote on my experiences as a neighbourhood community worker. Ten years later community work, or what can be seen as community work, is mainly not neighbourhood work, though I still believe that the best way of describing it is to use 'the neighbourhood model', which is what I have done. In the 1990s, however, the challenge is to adapt the model, or rather, the skills and value system underlying it to a range of different settings and to the far-reaching institutional changes which took place during the 1980s.

Readers who know me and my writing will also perhaps note a changed emphasis on ideology. I had always resisted neo-Marxist approaches to practice because they often seemed to suggest approaches to action which I 'knew' from my experience would not work, and appeared to devalue a lot of the good practical community work I saw going on around me. However, two things have changed: the first being myself. I am now considerably more sympathetic to Marxist or perhaps socialist feminist interpretations of how Western society came to exist in its present form, though I am still sceptical of some of the approaches to practice which are often taken to flow from that broad perspective. Second, however, there seems to me to be a much greater realism within those whose roots are in this 'radical' tradition, about how to go about practice in a way which brings results. Thus, I have attempted in this edition to synthesise, albeit in a modest way, what I had previously seen as contending approaches to community work.

This book is intended primarily for those who have done little community work, who want to know what it is and how they might go about it. There are also fairly extensive suggestions for further reading where I have indicated with some texts the main relevance, in my view, of what they have to say.

Many of the lessons I draw come from my own practice and from mistakes I have made, and I make no apology for this, since I think one learns best from making mistakes. Some readers may also consider that my tone is, in some places, a little pessimistic. That is not because I am pessimistic about community work: I am in fact very optimistic since I now see many people acknowledging the importance of community work skills, though they may not think of themselves as community workers. It is because the new worker often underestimates the difficulties in doing good community work that I have identified its difficulties. I have also emphasised apparently simple points, because in my experience it is often the simple things we forget and which cause the big problems rather than the complicated points.

I hope readers will use the book to develop their own ideas of what community work is rather than simply adopting, or rejecting, my model. I cannot tell you what community work is, only what it is for me, and perhaps for some other people, in the hope that this will help you work it out for yourself. If any reader would like to make any comments after reading the book I would very much like to receive them.

Most of my thanks go to people who need to be nameless; to those many people whose care and respect helped me grow during the last few years, also to those people who have disagreed with me and who may have forced me to rethink my ideas, to Peter Baldock, who as an 'anonymous' reviewer made several comments on the book, many of which I have incorporated, to Judith Bevan who made me realise that community workers can be rather a serious bunch and that we perhaps need to laugh at ourselves a bit more, and to Denise

Johns my loyal typist who actually says she misses poring over my ghastly handwriting if she does not receive a regular supply!

I have used 'she' almost entirely throughout, rather than 'he' because I believe that the language we use can sometimes serve to re-inforce sex role stereotyping.

ALAN TWELVETREES

1

What is Community Work?

Introduction

There is no agreement about what community work is. For the purposes of this book however I will define community work, at its simplest, as being the process of assisting ordinary people to improve their own communities by undertaking collective action. Providing this assistance often requires the employment of paid 'community workers' and it is their work which is the main focus of this book. However, these paid workers are employed in a number of different guises and may be called voluntary services officers, liaison officers, development workers, and the like, rather than community workers. They may also undertake a very wide range of functions, so that community work practice takes a great variety of forms. Here are just a few examples.

- A local authority employs a member of staff to ensure that community groups have good access to the council's decision-making procedures.
- A number of professional housing workers form a branch of the Campaign for the Homeless and Rootless.
- A community arts team organises street theatre and exhibitions involving a local community in exploring and celebrating its cultural roots.
- A member of staff in a women's refuge sets up a group where the members examine their experience of being women.

- An alliance of community groups and trades unionists runs a major campaign against cuts in public services.
- A common ownership development agency enables a group of redundant workers to form a producer co-operative.
- A social services department employs staff to enable people with a mental handicap to re-enter the community.
- A school involves pupils in a neighbourhood tree planting scheme and in visiting elderly people.
- A community organisation tenders for a contract to run the refuse collection service in its neighbourhood.
- A tenants' association forms itself into a housing co-operative which takes over and manages its own housing estate.

These kinds of enterprises share a concern to ensure first, that ordinary people, as residents, or as members of high need groups (such as people with a mental handicap) get a better deal, and, second, that they bring this 'better deal' about themselves, at least as far as is possible.

In order to make sense of the many different forms of community work it is most helpful, I think, to start with the *neighbourhood model*. At its simplest, the task of a neighbourhood community worker is to get to know how the residents of a small geographical area perceive the needs of their neighbourhood and to help them form groups which they run to improve it. Thus, when I was a neighbourhood worker I helped people set up and run a tenants' association, a carnival committee, an anti-motorway action group, an age concern group, a disabled association and other such groups.

The main rationale for employing staff to facilitate the development of such groups is twofold. First, a progressive and healthy society needs the active participation of its citizens in a wide variety of ways. Urban renewal almost always fails, for instance, when it is undertaken over the heads of local people. Almost no social service will run really effectively without some form of participation by the consumers of the service. Citizen participation is also needed, in my view, as a means of holding politicians and policy-makers to account. Second, without assistance many attempts of ordinary people to engage in collective action and other forms of participation fail, especially in communitiies which arguably need it most, such as run-down council estates. Therefore, ways need to be found of promoting this collective action.

However, community workers, whose main job is to promote this collective action, undertake many other activities besides offering support to community groups, and there are in fact a number of different approaches to community work. It is important to try to categorise these different approaches before examining practice in detail. It needs saying, however, that the messy reality of practice only approximates in general terms to these heuristic models or ideal types. The models serve to enhance our understanding of the world of community work, they do not describe it exactly.

Each category is listed below in the form of a bi-polar continuum. I then go on to explain them.

(a) *Radical* community work as opposed to *professional* community work.

(b) Community development approaches as opposed to social planning approaches.

(c) Self help or service strategies as opposed to influence (or campaigning) strategies.

(d) Generic community work as opposed to specialist community work.

(e) Concern about process as opposed to concern about product.

(f) The enabling as opposed to the organising role of the worker.

(g) Community work as an approach or attitude in other forms of work as opposed to community work in its own right.

(h) Unpaid community work as opposed to paid community work.

Radical and professional community work

Some people see community work as akin to a profession whereby paid workers, using specialist skills, enable community groups to run self help or campaigning activities and try to ensure that local authorities and other service providers deliver services more effectively so that they meet community needs better. I have called these people 'professional' community workers though this term oversimplifies a complex reality in order to make it intelligible. Such community workers may have a vision of a radically different society but nevertheless hold the view that community work can only contribute in a marginal way to the bringing about of that society. Or, they may believe that major societal change is either unnecessary or impossible. For them, community work meets enduring needs to do with seeking to empower disadvantaged people and trying to ensure a better fit between services and needs. 'Professional' community workers tend to be primarily concerned about skill development and practice theory and to emphasise the need to deal pragmatically in what they would see as the 'real world'. Writers such as Batten (1967), Biddle (1965), Goetschius (1969), Henderson and Thomas (1987) are good examples of this 'professional' tradition in community work, which was the main tradition from about 1945 until about 1970.

Other people whom I have, for simplicity, called 'radical' community workers, are passionately concerned to move from our present world to a radically different world, and, if possible, to use community work as a means of doing so. Drawing primarily on neo-Marxist and feminist analyses of present society they tend to emphasise that the present social and economic order operates by systematically oppressing certain groups, for instance the working class, women and ethnic minorities, and that this oppression is intrinsically tied up with the historical development of private property, the family, the class system and the state. 'Radical' community workers tend to believe that it is the task of the community worker to seek to create radical change in society. Therefore, it does not make sense to play by the accepted rules of the game. Such workers also tend to emphasise that a community work which sees itself as a profession operating within the constraints imposed by contemporary political structures and culture acts, in effect, to re-inforce the status quo. If, for instance, community workers are enabling community groups to participate in and benefit from the existing system they are likely to be reinforcing rather than changing that system.

For these reasons, community workers from this 'radical' tradition, which has its roots in the politics of dissent, have tended to search for 'oppositional' ways of working which challenge the status quo. In the early 1970s this often took the form of organising militant campaigns, seeking to build links with organisations such as trades unions, making propaganda, and seeking to get alternative issues on public agendas. In more recent years, particularly with the growing influence of feminist thought and Marxist writers such as Gramsci, community workers whose roots are in this radical tradition have acknowledged the importance of working to change ideas at least as well as structures. To take one example, some women's groups have concentrated on consciousness raising as a means of helping women, including the community workers, to develop images of themselves as people who act rather than who are acted upon.

In recognition of the fact that hierarchical structures tend to oppress the people in them workers belonging to the radical tradition have also tended to experiment with non-hierarchical organisations, where decisions are taken collectively, and where roles are shared as equally as possible. This is an attempt to 'prefigure' a more just and equal society, in recognition that if a different society were attained by the 'wrong' means it would be the wrong kind of society

Community workers whose roots are in the 'radical' tradition now tend to place great emphasis on anti-racist and anti-sexist work. They often also emphasise the 'social construction' of reality. They might argue that sex roles, bureaucratic organisation or capitalism, for instance, are social constructions, that these kinds of social relations only pertain by convention and that they can therefore be changed.

Sadly, discourse between the radical and the professional tradition has been problematic, since whether somebody belongs primarily to one rather than the other often comes down to very personal assumptions about the world – whether we believe ultimately that people will do the right thing if left alone, for example. These beliefs are often both unstated and insecure points of psychological anchorage in a world where we do not really know anything. Therefore, to hear somebody arguing in support of a position which depends upon our most basic assumptions being false is immensely threatening personally. In addition, if two people are disagreeing about the need for bureaucratic forms of organisation while their unstated and unexplored assumptions about human nature are strongly at variance, it is easy to see why no real discourse can take place. Each position may well be quite logical from the (unstated) premises from which its advocate started.

It needs emphasising that these two traditions, the professional and the radical are much oversimplified here. Many community workers draw on powerful insights from socialist/feminist theory and are concerned to explore alternative ways of working while at the same time acknowledging the need for coherent skill development and the necessity of operating in a pragmatic fashion in the world as it is today. Thus, the professional tradition and the radical tradition can best be seen, I think, as complementary ways of understanding and intervening in the world. They are sets of ideas upon which all community workers should be able to draw as and when they find them appropriate.

Community development and social planning

If we take the 'neighbourhood model' of community work we find that the worker usually operates in two main ways. The first way is, as I indicated above, to help people form groups which they themselves run. Thus the worker is in a general sense promoting *self help* even if that self help involves a group campaigning to influence an organisation outside the community, such as the local authority. This approach to community work can most usefully be called the community development approach, and it is this form of work which is most characteristic of community work. In its classic form the community development approach emphasises the objectivity of the worker and implies she will work 'non-directively' with people on what *they* decide to become involved with. It tends to assume a homogeneous or unified community, and implies that the community will use or create its own resources to meet its needs. It also tends to imply a co-operative government somewhat in the background and consensual methods of problem solving. I have deliberately caricatured the community development approach in order to accentuate it as an 'ideal type' since, in reality, pure community development is difficult to find. In its idealised form this community development model clearly underplays differences within the community (and in wider society) based on class, race or age for instance, and differences between the community and the outside world, where private developers are 'developing' an area in ways which do not benefit local people for instance.

The second type of approach involves the community worker liaising and working directly with policy-makers and service providers to improve services or alter policies. This form of community work is most usefully called the social planning approach. While, in my view, all community workers need to be able to work in both kinds of ways – with politicians, local government officers and, increasingly, business people, as well as with local people – some community work jobs will involve more opportunities for community development and others more opportunities for social planning.

There are also many forms of community work which involve both community development and social planning. For instance an 'umbrella' organisation for a neighbourhood may consist of representatives both from community groups and the local authority. Thus, a community worker who was servicing this group would be involved in community development and in social planning as she would be working with both 'community people' and service providers. Similarly a community worker employed in a housing department to involve public sector tenants in housing policy decisions would inevitably also do a great deal of work with policy-makers.

The twin concepts of community development and social planning are taken from a seminal article by Rothman (1976).

However, he uses the term 'locality development' rather than community development. I think 'locality development' is too narrow a term, since community workers are often now not neighbourhood workers. They work increasingly, with 'communities of interest', women, ethnic minorities, or homeless people for instance, or they work on particular issues – arts, employment, housing, for example – rather than with any group on any issue in a small scale geographical community. That is why my version is 'community development' and not locality development.

Rothman has a third model which he calls social action. I deal both with communities of interest and with social action below.

Service approaches and influence approaches

So far, we have concentrated on the role of the community worker or the community work agency. Now we shift to the role of the community group or organisation with which the worker is working. Simply put, some needs can be met from the resources existing within the community or at least with limited support from outside the community. Social events, play-schemes, youth clubs, lunch clubs for older people, voluntary visiting schemes, alcoholics anonymous groups, some educational classes, even in certain situations the building of a community centre and some aspects of job creation would all come into this category. In these types of situations the group is involved in a 'service' strategy using primarily the resources of the community (though it can also be seen as a self help strategy).

Other needs can only be met by modifying or changing the policies of organisations outside the community. These kinds of needs require 'influence' strategies, which can involve collaboration, campaigning, 'contest' and civil disobedience. (See chapter 6 for a more detailed discussion of different kinds of influence strategies.)

Generic and specialist community work

Some neighbourhood workers are able to work on any issue –
play, employment, leisure, housing and so on – whatever kind
of agency they work for. Such workers can be called generic
workers. Because they do not have responsibility to deliver a
particular service they are relatively free to work from the
'bottom up' in helping people articulate their needs and to
come together to see that these are met.

However, the 'generic', 'bottom up' worker operating in a
small scale geographical community is a dying breed because
there is no funding agency with a central responsibility for
neighbourhood community development. On the other hand,
almost every service agency one can think of needs both to
improve its services to its clients or consumers and, in order to
do that, to involve them in the development of the service.
For instance, if one considers the process by which
community care for older people, people with disabilities or
other high need groups is to be improved, this must involve
the community and the consumers in a wide range of ways.
Similarly the police need to involve the community in crime
prevention just as housing departments need to involve
tenants in various aspects of housing policy. The list is
endless. These service agencies are increasingly appointing
specialist community workers (though they would usually
have other job titles) whose jobs are, first, to extend and
improve services and, second to involve the consumers, often
at a minimal level, in this process (see Willmott, 1989). Thus,
over the last decade there has been a growing emphasis on
what can be called specialist community work with communities of interest on specific issues rather than generic work in
geographical communities.

While this 'specialised' community work could in theory be
primarily 'bottom up' it is usually centred on the needs of
agencies rather than on the needs of the community as
articulated by its members (at least in statutory agencies).
Thus, it tends to be top down work (social planning) with only
small amounts of 'bottom up' work (community development). Indeed, some 'agency centred' initiatives (for example
planning consultations) may be undertaken primarily to

ensure that the services the agency wants to develop are not opposed by the consumer! Thus consumer participation can be seen as a means of service providers legitimising what they want to do anyway and in some cases, diverting attention away from intractable problems.

As Willmott points out, 'top down' initiatives to involve the community can only work if 'bottom up' initiatives also exist, but the resources are not usually devoted by the statutory agencies to promoting 'bottom up' initiatives. While service led or top down initiatives are important they need to be properly resourced (which they usually are not), and they are, in my view, no substitute for the 'bottom up' work which is more truly people-centred.

When one looks at areas where community work is fairly well developed, it is evident that there now exist in many places specialist support agencies. These include resources centres which offer reprographic services, information, advice on fund-raising or legal matters and other technical services, adult education centres which offer courses in welfare rights, housing law or committee work, play associations which can advise groups on the establishment of summer play-schemes, and volunteer bureaux which act as employment exchanges for volunteers, to name but a few. However, while these agencies do resource community action, they still tend to lack staff with the skill and time to do the outreach work in which community development workers specialise and which is necessary to involve the uninvolved.

Broady and Hedley (1989) stress that local authorities engage in a range of activities which involve liaison with the community and which the local authorities often call community development, but which do not fit the 'bottom up' definition of community development. These activities can include liaison with parish councils, the provision of community facilities, decentralising services, enabling the community to manage community centres, providing grants to voluntary groups and setting up neighbourhood committees. These approaches seem to me to include elements of both specialist and generic community development, but also large elements of social planning.

The other point to emerge clearly from Broady and

Hedley's book is that local authorities cannot really dabble in community work to any real effect. The need to develop coherent policies towards it. Willmott's research bears this out in that he concludes that such top down community initiatives are often ill thought out, under-resourced, under-evaluated, and, sometimes, of doubtful value.

Process and product

Process goals are to do with changes in people's confidence, knowledge, technical skills or attitudes. Product goals are to do with the changed material situation – an improved home help service or a successful play-scheme. Both sets of goals are important throughout community work and both are intertwined. For some community workers process goals predominate and product goals are secondary. Other workers are primarily concerned about product goals and see the development of skills in the community as a means to that end. While most workers are concerned with both types of goal, workers of different tendencies may emphasise different types of process goals and product goals. 'Radical' community workers may be more concerned with politicisation and social action strategies for instance while 'professional' community workers may be more concerned about skill development, self help and service strategies.

Different situations also tend to dictate whether process goals or product goals predominate. I was once working with a group to try to prevent a motorway from being built. In order to present evidence at the public enquiry a great deal of co-ordinated work had to be undertaken quickly. If process goals had predominated and attention had been given to ensuring that the group members developed the skills to run this kind of campaign the deadline would have been missed.

Community work is predicated on the central idea, that product goals are brought about by a process which ensures that the participants in the action have as much control as possible over all its aspects and that they acquire an enduring capacity to act themselves as a result. However, this educational process usually only works if product goals are

net, since group members lose heart if they fail to
e their objectives. Therefore, in most situations
workers have to give attention to both kinds of goals.

Some community groups are only concerned with process,
and we call these 'expressive' groups. They include educational, social, recreational and support groups, where the sole
purpose of the group is the shared experience and the
learning within it. Expressive groups can be contrasted with
instrumental groups where the main purpose is to organise
some collective action outside the group, running a
newsletter or mounting a demonstration, for example. These
instrumental groups are essentially committees, though they
may not seem to be.

While all groups have expressive functions, in that the
members gain or fail to gain from the social interaction in a
meeting, some groups have no instrumental functions. It is
important for a worker to understand the main function of a
group since an instrumental group needs members who can
run meetings and organise action, that is, leaders, at least as
well as people who could obtain some benefit from being
members but who could not contribute towards product
goals.

Worker role

The classic community development role is that of enabler,
guide, catalyst or facilitator. This style of work is also
sometimes called 'non-directive'. However, there are times
when the worker may take a leadership role within a group, as
chair, secretary, or even 'fixer' or 'trouble shooter', because
product goals predominate and the group members may lack
the necessary skills, at a particular time.

When acting in the social planning mode the worker tends
to take on the role of expert or advocate, though workers who
undertake social planning roles also need to work towards
changing the attitudes of power holders which may also mean
playing the role of facilitator. It also needs saying that
community workers spend more time with individuals than
within groups. Indeed, while groups are needed because they

have more power and legitimacy than individuals, much of the learning which happens as a result of community work takes place largely through one to one interactions.

Community work as an attitude or approach

Both specialist and generic community work are forms of community work in its own right. But the central ideas which are to do with empowering the consumer, understanding community needs and taking these into account when policy is made, are not unique to community work. Indeed, good management, industrial relations, relations between family members, and relations between all professionals and consumers need, it seems to me, to reflect this ethos if they are to be effective.

Unpaid community work

There is no monopoly on the term community work, nor should there be. Many people who are active in their own communities, in trades unions, as elected representatives, as committee members of voluntary organisations and so on might claim to be community workers, though they are unpaid. The main difference between paid and unpaid community work is, however, that the unpaid workers are usually leaders, organisers, activists, rather than, primarily, persons who support the unpaid work of others. That distinguishes, for me, paid from unpaid community work and again emphasises the core (paid) community work role of being a facilitator.

Starting where people are

Stories like the following one abound in community work. Two community workers on a council housing estate were keen to set up a tenants' association to pressurise the council to repair the council housing more effectively. Tenants seemed interested and agreed to come to a meeting to discuss it. Nobody came. The workers organised two other meetings and the total attendance was one person. Then, some tenants asked the workers to help them set up a bingo group. While the tenants, presumably, wanted better housing it looked as if they were not motivated to take collective action to do anything about it, at least at that time. The workers had allowed their own judgements about what could most benefit the estate at that particular time to prevent them perceiving that the tenants were not where they, the community workers 'were at'.

This is the central paradox of community work. On the one hand it can only work if the members of the community take prime responsibility for, and thus 'own', the action which takes place. On the other hand, what the members of the community want to do is often very different from what the community workers think they should do! There are strong parallels here with social work. There is some evidence to suggest that, if people are 'given' social work when they do not want it, this can be harmful, and that social work is only effective when a worker is helping a client work on something that the client has identified that he or she wants to work on (see especially Raynor, 1985; but also Rogers, 1961).

A community worker who thinks the community has a particular need but finds that, at a particular time, the community will not work to achieve it has a simple, if painful choice. On the one hand she can seek to achieve it herself (by taking a social planning approach or by taking a leadership role in the community) which runs against the core principle of enabling 'community people' to take leadership roles. On the other hand she can wait and 'sow seeds' until the community or some people in it, are ready to 'own' what she thinks they should own. She might in such a situation also work with the community on priorities it identified but which were not hers. This paradox is complicated in practice because, as community workers, we are often so enthusiastic about our own objectives for the community that we fail to perceive that the community members do not share that enthusiasm or will attend meetings only if somebody else (for example the community worker) leads. This mistake is easy to make, partly because community members will often tell a worker what they think she wants to hear. It is this paradox which makes community work so difficult. Yet the uniqueness of community work derives from a value system which emphasises the importance of people discovering what they want to do, doing it, and not having it imposed on them.

How to go about doing that is the focus of the remainder of this book.

2

The Community Development Process I: Contact-making, Analysis and Planning

Introduction

In considering the notion 'community' Willmott (1989) emphasises two main points. First, communities can either be of a geographical nature, or they can be 'communities of interest' where the link between people is something other than locality. This link can be as diverse as belonging to the same ethnic minority, being a woman, supporting the same football club or having a particular kind of handicap. Second, there is both attachment and interaction between the members of a community. I will use the term community of interest to describe these non-geographical communities both where they already exist or where they potentially exist, in that interaction and attachment are not yet present.

Community workers are now concerned as much with communities based on shared race or with people who have particular problems in common, homeless people, drug users, women suffering domestic violence and people with handicaps, as they are with small scale geographical communities. People with particular problems or disabilities are often isolated from each other and it is sometimes the job of the community worker to bring them together, and, in a certain sense, to help them form communities.

The needs and problems which are specific to each community or potential community and the legislation relating to it significantly affect the way in which a community worker operates. Thus, at first sight the differences between doing community development with cancer sufferers and with unemployed people seeking to create producer co-operatives, or between doing it with the parents of mentally handicapped children and with women suffering domestic violence seem to outweigh the similarities. However, this is largely because it is easier to be aware of the specific characteristics of the particular 'community' and the need to understand these than it is to identify the universal principles of community development, which apply in each case.

A community worker must be able to think through the possible implications of any actions she takes. The following is an example of where I once got it wrong. As a lecturer in community work I had arranged to see a county councillor, along with the assistant county clerk, in order to discuss future student placements in a resource centre of which the councillor was the chair. The purpose of the meeting, from my point of view, was to discuss placements in general and to establish a good relationship with the councillor, so that the student, whom I took along to the meeting, would not encounter difficulties with him. We had a friendly discussion and managed to convey to the councillor that the placement was not intended to threaten his authority. All was well, or so I thought, until the student's supervisor rang me. He was most unhappy that I had met the councillor 'behind his back', and said he would now have to reconsider taking the student on placement. I had been so concerned about the county councillor that I had failed to consider adequately how other parties might feel. If I had stopped and thought about who else might be affected by such a meeting I might have gone about it differently. This failure to think through the possible outcomes of our actions is common in community work, and can only be avoided if we structure into our job a means of analysing, examining alternatives and possible outcomes before acting, and of working out our objectives as clearly as possible, as well as consciously evaluating our work.

Contact-making – our bread and butter

The key to good practice is contact-making. The reasons are as follows. First, to get anything done we need to build an alliance with other people. But besides the relatively few people with whom we will have an alliance to achieve a particular objective, we need the support and goodwill of as many other people as possible. Unless we take care to cultivate this goodwill and mutual understanding widely, we may find that the natural conservatism and resistance to change of most people will turn into opposition to us and our proposals. Therefore, it is necessary initially to establish contacts with people of like mind. We cannot know who has the time, inclination, resources, and connections needed to undertake a successful piece of action unless we are continually making and remaking contacts at all levels in a systematic way. Second, community work could be described as permanent innovation. We need to be constantly on the lookout, not only for people with whom an alliance can be built, but also for new ideas and new ways of looking at problems. This creative process occurs principally when one is in regular contact with a wide range of people. Then it is possible to pick up different ideas, see how they fit with one's own, try them out on third parties, and put these people, as appropriate, into contact with each other. Here is an example of how this can happen.

We had never had much contact with the probation office in the area in which I worked, but by chance I had supervised one of the officers now working in the area when he was a student. When chatting one day we came to the view that it might be a good idea for our team to meet their team. We arranged a meeting during which they expressed concern that probationers in the locality had to travel a long way across town to report to the office. After further discussion we arranged to make a room available in our neighbourhood centre once a week for the probation office to use as a reporting centre.

But is not contact-making just common sense? Perhaps it is, but common sense is not that common! By trial and error I found that the most important principles or rules to follow are these:

Rule 1:   Never pass up the opportunity to make or renew a contact – unless you are fairly sure that to do so at this point will damage another area of work. Also, it is not usually a good idea to ask a new contact for something you want at the first meeting. Concentrate more on finding out how she sees the situation and what her self interest is.

Rule 2: Consider first and foremost what impression you are making. How we dress, for instance, is a statement about ourselves and people automatically make assumptions about us from it. Consider whether you are having the effect on the other person that you want to have.

Punctuality is vital, and many social and community workers are very casual in this respect. People in authority may write us off before we start if we turn up half an hour late for the first meeting. Equally, people will not take us seriously if we agree to do something and fail to do it. Say well in advance if you are not able to honour a commitment. We need to be seen as a credible person with as many people as possible because we may at some stage want their help. This is equally important when dealing with those who are diametrically opposed to what we are doing, because if we are in conflict with them they are more likely to think carefully before fighting us.

Rule 3: Learn how to listen and notice. By 'listening' I am referring not only to the process of taking in the explicit content of what someone says but also to understanding what may only be implied. Is the person just saying what she thinks you want to hear? What is she conveying about her relationships with other residents or her family, or in the case of a local government official, other departments? Most important of all, for initial contacts with community members, what are they conveying about both their motivation and their ability to take organisational responsibility?

If we are listening to another person talk we do not only use our ears. We speak too, and it may often be necessary to prompt in order to bring the other person round to discussing matters we want to discuss. Good listening is the art of first registering the explicit and implicit content of what a person says and second, assessing or interpreting it, perhaps tentatively at first. Good listening does not mean we do not contribute. Neither does it mean we cannot at least partly structure what happens.

Listening to ourselves is, if anything, more important than listening to others. Following Rogers (1961) I am increasingly convinced that we cannot perceive others accurately unless we are in touch with our own feelings. Do we actually find this person boring, do we find we become angry when she is talking? Do we feel threatened? It is also important to try to understand what the other person is feeling, to put ourselves in her place. Whatever we want from the meeting – information, a relationship, money, even an understanding of the other's weak points, we are more likely to go about getting it in appropriate ways if we can empathise in this way.

We have to train ourselves to notice not only how we affect other people, but also how they in turn react to other parties. At the meeting with the county councillor to which I referred earlier, the assistant county clerk said virtually nothing and looked bored. That indicated something to me about the relationship between the councillor and that officer, a point useful for me to know at a later date perhaps. A great deal can be learnt by noticing where people sit, how they arrange their offices and rooms, what newspaper they read, what pictures they have on the wall, and so on. For many of us this means practice, it does not come naturally. Neighbourhood community workers also need to notice what is going on in the locality. If people appear with theodolites a community worker should go and ask them what they are doing – it may be the first sign that a new road scheme is being considered. It is useful to know what shops are closing, who frequents which pub, what houses are vacant; in short, indications of the small and sometimes not so small changes that are continually taking place in a locality. It is also important to check the local paper for applications for planning permission and local authority proposals for the area.

Community workers also need to guard against becoming too parochial. Workers doing similar jobs in other parts of the country will have discovered many ways of dealing with situations which you are meeting for the first time. So, find ways of learning from them.

Rule 4: Create opportunities for establishing personal contacts. For neighbourhood community workers the rule could be rephrased thus: *Walk don't ride.* If a worker wishes to make contacts and to notice changes it is good practice for her to walk around the area. Walking around one's area is a means of structuring contact-making. There are of course times when it is more appropriate to walk than others, in summer for instance, and it is important to plan contact-making accordingly. The same principle applies to community workers operating above neighbourhood level. They need to put themselves in situations where they have time to meet their clientele casually and informally, but in a systematic way.

Rule 5: In order to get we must give. This is not just a rule for community work, it is a rule for life. Most of us often have a mixture of uncomfortable feelngs when we meet people for the first time, particularly people whose objectives are not clear to us and who may want something from us. How do *you* deal with a door-to-door salesman or an evangelist from a religious sect for example? Community workers are in many ways just the same as salesmen or evangelists, but we may be more devious about the product we wish to sell!

A worker's first meeting with a councillor or a local resident may reveal a range of communication problems and needs to be handled with some care. For instance, the councillor may feel that the worker is a threat, that any information she provides may be used against her. Local residents may feel uncomfortable if the worker is vague about what her purpose is and who employs her, and may well be suspicious of somebody without a clear function who just says she wants to help the community.

When working with communities of interest it is usually necessary for the worker to state who she is at first – 'I'm from Social Services and . . .'. However, some neighbourhood workers say they prefer not to reveal at an early stage the agency they work for and their objectives. I normally feel constrained to convey to the other person as soon as possible where I come from and what I want. Perhaps this is because I expect this from people who are meeting me for the first time. When contact-making in a casual setting, in a pub for example, this may not be so necessary. But as soon as we begin to suggest that our contact takes some action then I believe we should convey who we are and why we are there.

We may not feel too happy that we work for the Social Services department because we think that our contact may have had a bad experience in previous dealings with the organisation. But sooner or later she must know, and it helps other people to place us in context if they know where we come from.

In most meetings our purpose is to motivate the other person to action, if only to provide us with information. But people do not give us what we want for nothing. They give best if they get something in return. We usually have to let them talk first about what interests them: their work, their hobbies, their family perhaps. Most important, we have to be genuinely interested in them. Once I contacted the headmaster of the local school shortly after he took up his post. I explained what I was doing and made tactful suggestions that he and his staff might get more involved in the community. Nothing doing! Many months later he complained to me that parents would not visit the school on open evenings. I listened patiently for some time and eventually asked if he thought they might come to our neighbourhood centre if a teacher was available there. He became interested and eventually an agreement was made to use our centre. Only when I could help him was he prepared to listen to me.

Often, community workers appreciate the importance of relationship skills, particularly the skill of empathy, when contacting people in the community, but forget the importance of these skills with officials, whom they expect to be remote, unforthcoming and even antagonistic to any community work initiative. Officials and councillors have sensitive feelings too, and if we go into meetings with the expectation that officials will not be helpful, and if we are not prepared to work at building relationships with them, our expectations of antagonism and a lack of co-operation will become self-fulfilling. It is useful also to have a strategy prepared in case someone is obstructive! Do your homework and think about the likely reaction of the other person before the meeting and plan various possible ways of handling the situation.

Rule 6:   Do not believe everything people say. If I listen to a lecture which has some good points and some poor points and

the lecturer later asks me what I thought of it, I am m/
to mention the good points. If I then discuss it witn ?
party who emphasises the bad points, I may agree with what
this person says. In neither conversation could it be said I am
being dishonest. We often tell a person only half of what we
are feeling. Very often a member of a community group
would tell me privately that she was going to resign very soon,
but never actually did so. While she was talking to me it might
have been her full intention to resign because she was
particularly aware at that moment of the frustrations of being
a member of the group. But at other times she would have
looked at her membership of the group in different ways and
become more aware of the disadvantages of leaving, so when
it came to the crunch she would not resign. When I had been
around for a little time I no longer automatically believed
what people told me. I stored the information and waited to
see whether it was corroborated by information from other
sources or whether intentions did indeed become action.
Many people will also lie about the facts of a situation in order
to save face when under pressure, or will assert the opposite
of what is actually the case because they want to convince us
that they 'always consult widely', for instance.

A community profile   *Read this over.*

Purpose

Before acting it is vital to get as much relevant information as
possible, upon which to base our actions. The purpose of a
community profile is first, to gather *information* about the
needs of a locality and the potential for action and second, to
provide the basis for an *analysis* of possible alternative
courses of action from which to choose priorities. However,
in the process of gathering the relevant information we make
contact with many people, and some of those contacts are
likely to be the starting-point for action. We may discover
that several local people are concerned about the lack of
play-space and are prepared to do something about it, for
example. The community profile stage may then overlap with

the action stage, because, although we must have an overall plan, we must also take opportunities when they arise. We are also likely to be under external and internal pressure to come up quickly with evidence of our work. Therefore, the tendency is to omit or skimp the community profile. This is particularly dangerous when we succeed another worker. I never carried out a community profile when I started out as a neighbourhood worker. I worked largely from the basis of contacts left by my predecessor and never forced myself to stand back when starting the job, review my overall strategy, or to develop my own contacts. I made many mistakes as a result, such as setting up a tenants' association which nobody wanted.

Two types of information are required for a community profile, hard and soft. Hard information consists of quantifiable and quantified data, and can be obtained from official reports such as the census. Soft information is more subjective and consists largely of opinions. On the one hand, it is no good understanding housing statistics relating to the locality unless we know the views of residents about their housing needs. On the other hand it would not be the wisest course of action to try to set up an organisation for one-parent families without making an attempt to ascertain the approximate number of such families in the first place. There is an excellent booklet entitled *A Guide to the Assessment of Community Needs and Resources* (Glampson *et al.*, 1975) which indicates the information needed for a community profile and how to go about getting it. See also Henderson and Thomas (1987).

Gathering information in the worker's own agency

Even before she starts work a community worker is usually given some idea about what at least some people in the agency expect her to do. This is increasingly the case today where there are clearer expectations about what a community worker should achieve, rather than an 'open-ended' job description. However, the job as defined may well not be workable. Moreover, different colleagues may well have differing expectations of the worker. So their different views have to be carefully considered. At the same time as establishing relationships with colleagues it is necessary to read any relevant records and to discover whether the agency keeps any hard data which will be of use. Very soon, however, a problem crops up. The information may not be compiled in such a way as to break down as easily as is required. We then have to decide whether the data are so important that we are prepared to spend time going back to the original sources.

It is also important to look at past reports containing proposals for the area. By doing this we are developing a sense of the agency's history in relation to that area, which is crucial in making the right judgement as far as action is concerned. If we know how the area has been perceived over time we should be able to predict more accurately how the agency will react to our own proposals. We must know whether a certain approach was once tried and failed. It is important also to look at relevant planning documents. Planning sections of local authorities will often make these available, together with other statistical data. It is important to contact these officials and ask them about what relevant information exists if one does not already know. They are usually pleased to help. It is also necessary to acquire from colleagues in the agency their perception not only of needs in the area, but also their views of the agency: who holds power, who to go through to get things done, who is sympathetic to your approach, who to get on your side. It is important to talk to a range of people, not just social workers but home-help organisers, for example, to obtain views from different levels, and particularly from people who may be sceptical about community work. All this gives you a broader base for your analysis. At the same time, it is necessary to ask them if they can suggest further contacts in other organisations or in the target community. By this process we establish our own network of contacts. But we also need to be clear as to *why* we are going to see someone. An interview is frustrating for both sides if neither party knows why it is taking place.

Gathering hard information

It is useful to know the size and age structure of the population and other demographic data. Some of this information will be in the census which should be in the public library. It is useful also, to be able to work out trends, whether the black population, for example, is increasing, which may mean referring to previous censuses as well. It could also help to know, for instance, how the figures for infant mortality compare with the area as a whole and with Britain as a whole. The first can be obtained from the census, the second from *Social Trends*. But we should use our own initiative too. School rolls will provide information about the child population, and it might be possible to find a head teacher, who can provide information which reveals year-to-year changes which a census does not. It is also necessary to know the socio-economic class structure and unemployment rates for men, women and school leavers. Again the census will be of use.

An understanding of the local economic structure is basic in analysing the needs and problems of a community. It is useful to know where people work, and, particularly, if they tend to live near where they work or not, what kind of pay they get, whether the firms use high or low technology, whether they are contracting or expanding, whether they depend on orders from larger firms, whether they are investing in new plant. This helps to develop a general feeling about the industrial scene. The local authority economic development department ought to be able to provide some useful information in this respect.

It will be necessary to discover whether the housing is public or private, its age, the degree to which houses contain basic facilities, the degree of overcrowding, and patterns of multi-occupation. Information about the local authority's housing policies may also be useful; their allocation and transfer policies, for example. The planning and housing departments could, if willing, provide this information. Housing committee minutes and the annual reports of the housing manager to the council may be of use too.

It is important to find out which councillors represent particular wards, who are the 'heavyweight' councillors and who sit on the most important committees. How strong are the various political parties on the council? Has one party been in power for a long time or have there been changes?

Much of this information can be obtained from the town hall information office and the rest from speaking with friendly politicians, officials or activists who have been around for a long time. It can be useful to observe a full council meeting or a committee.

Information also needs to be obtained about all statutory agencies which are located in or serve the area; health centres, police, educational welfare officers, youth centres, public transport and other services such as refuse collection. Whenever possible it is useful to go and see the relevant personnel in these agencies rather than merely finding out about them at secondhand.

Non-statutory organisations are so many and varied that they are difficult to categorise. There are voluntary organisations employing professionals, such as the National Society for the Prevention of Cruelty to Children. There are commercial voluntary organisations like working-men's clubs and commercially run opportunities for leisure-time pursuits, such as cinemas and bingo halls. There are also churches, other religious organisations and political organisations. Finally there is a plethora of voluntary organisations which are the bread and butter of neighbourhood community workers, tenants' associations and play groups, for example, and more traditional voluntary organisations such as the Women's Royal Voluntary Service and organisations for people with a physical handicap which may well be part of a national structure. This information can be discovered mainly by asking around and exploring the area. The public library may also be able to help.

To find out what it is like to be a resident in a particular locality it is often quite a good idea to behave like one for a day; to travel across town by bus or approach estate agents about accommodation. If you are working in a disadvantaged area try to find ways of getting a real feel of what it is like to be a person living there.

In obtaining this information we meet a wide range of people, and we need to take advantage of these contacts to build up our stock of soft information. What do they think are the needs of the area? What is their position in their organisation? What are the pet schemes they want to back?

What are they touchy about? What are they afraid of? At this stage in our work we should also be recording the information we obtain fairly conscientiously, because the next stage is to try to marry it all together into an analysis which will lead to action.

Gathering information from residents

Our contacts with other professionals may provide us with the names of several people who are or were active in community organisations, and it is important to follow up these contacts. Introducing ourselves may not be too difficult because we can usually mention the person who referred us to them. Nevertheless we have to think about how we describe ourselves. It is accurate but rather vague and often inappropriate at an initial meeting to say that we have come to help them join with other residents in taking action on issues they are concerned about. But over time we need to find ways of conveying this, perhaps by giving examples of concrete ways in which we could help. Often the best way is to engage them in general conversation and gradually slip in the points we want to make. At this stage, however, we are mainly wanting general information: we want to pick their brains about the history of community action in the area and what is currently going on; we want to know how they perceive needs and problems; we want to know if they can put us in touch with other people who are concerned about the needs of the locality and who can give us more information. This process of building up contacts one from the other is sometimes called 'snowballing'.

While we may wish to encourage some of the local people whom we contact to become involved in community action, it is important not to be too 'pushy'. Attempting to 'push' people into community action before they are ready may frighten them off for ever. At this stage the worker is a student; she is learning.

Many people are quite pleased to talk about themselves and the problem is often stopping them! Another problem may be to keep them on the general subject of community needs rather than more personal concerns. Yet on the other hand we have to allow people to talk about what *they* want in order to establish a relationship. If a community worker considers that public transport is inadequate, based on her own analysis of needs, she might introduce the subject by asking whether it is easy to get into town and back. That way she is guiding the discussion but not imposing a rigid structure. An opportunity may also occur for the worker to demonstrate her commitment. If, for example, the contact says there used to be a playgroup run by Mrs X but since it closed the equipment seems to have got lost, the worker could offer to visit Mrs X to try to discover the whereabouts of the equipment. Actions like this are often more important in conveying what the worker is there for than mere words. At the same time she has to take care that she does not spring too quickly into action, thus neglecting her strategic planning tasks and giving the impression that she is there to do things *for* people rather than to help them do things themselves.

The danger with building up contacts one from another is that we may become familiar with only one network, since people will often put us in contact with their friends, or people who have the same views. Thus, it is important to make contacts in other ways too, by attending places where people naturally congregate, outside primary schools at the end of the school day, for instance. Other commonly used places are pubs, bus stops, or launderettes, but there are many more possibilities. However, when making contacts by going to places where people naturally congregate, one is meeting with an unrepresentative group: women with young children, for example. Are the people one is meeting representative enough? Other factors affect this type of contact-making too. Some female community workers feel unhappy chatting alone to men in public houses. On the other hand, some workers might be drawn to using public houses as a means of making contacts because of their liking of a pub atmosphere rather than because this was the best way of getting to know people. Like everything else we do in community work it is important to think about the methods we choose to make these contacts.

Planned door-knocking is another method to consider. However, it takes a great deal of time. If a worker wants open-ended discussions with as many residents as possible, she is likely to be in some houses for well over an hour. If she has to return later to houses where the occupant is initially out, it can take weeks to contact even half of the residents in a street. I once asked a student on placement to make contacts in this way in a street of 200 houses. It took about half of her three-month placement and resulted initially in two major contacts, one of whom fairly quickly left the area.

One way for a worker to ease the first meeting with people when door-knocking is to put a leaflet through the door a day or so before she calls, stating who she is and what her business is. It is amazing how this can break the ice.

Contact-making does not necessarily produce quick or direct results. People participate when *they* are ready. The fact that a community worker has contacted them at a certain point may well provide them with more knowledge than they had before. She may have sown seeds which begin to germinate at a later date, perhaps next year when their children go to school and they have a little more time on their hands, for example. It is also important not to make up our minds about people too quickly. A student on placement made an initially favourable contact with a vicar who promised a lot of help. On the other hand a local councillor was very suspicious and was mentally 'written off' by the student. Later the vicar showed himself only interested in getting people into church but the councillor became most helpful when she realised that the worker had a genuine commitment to the area. Many of the people with real power and commitment will not co-operate until a worker has shown herself trustworthy. We really do have to discover what people themselves want before we can involve them effectively. They will not stay involved unless what they want to do coincides with what we want them to do.

Another way to discover the felt needs of residents is to use a survey. Many of the comments made on door-knocking also apply here, particularly that it is a very time-consuming. Above all, it is important to work out beforehand whether the survey is being used as a means of getting into houses and gathering 'soft' information more systematically, or whether the task is to produce a more objective measurement of need.

Many community workers think they can do both at once, which is difficult. An objective survey must be carefully designed, especially if it is to cover intangible areas such as attitudes. It will need to be closed-ended, with questions like: 'Do you mainly shop in this street/in this estate/in town/ elsewhere?' The interviewer's task is to get clear answers to questions which can then be quantified. But if a worker is using the survey as a means of contacting residents and building up her store of soft information she will want to encourage respondents to talk at some length around the questions she asks. Thus she will ask 'open-ended' questions such as 'What do you think of the shops in the area?' Both types of survey are useful but it is important to know which approach, or which combination of the two, is most appropriate to the task in hand. See Thomas (1976, pp. 77–8) for some further comments on the use of surveys. If a worker opts for a survey to provide herself with an accurate picture of need rather than the 'soft' variety, she should make sure she gets an expert on surveys to help her. The nearest university or polytechnic should be able to assist.

An 'issue' profile

Henderson and Thomas (1987) discuss undertaking a 'broad angle' scan followed by a 'narrow angle' scan when discovering information. This is necessary because even in a generic community work project there will be some existing expectations that the worker will work on certain issues rather than others. The broad angle scan provides limited general information about the locality. The narrow angle scan provides more detailed information relevant to the specific areas of work in which the worker expects to be involved. It is important to distinguish between the two because one can go on gathering information about a geographical area for ever, and it is necessary to undertake a community profile as economically as possible. If, for instance, both hard and soft information obtained in the broad angle scan suggest that there are large numbers of children with nothing to do in the locality and the agency's terms of reference cover children as well as other groups a narrow angle scan might usefully concentrate on obtaining more information about the needs of children and how they could most effectively be met.

With a community of interest the community profile (which I prefer to call an issue profile in this context) has no geographical meaning, except in the loose sense that the worker will be operating across a city or a county, for example. But the principles for undertaking it are the same as for a geographical profile, namely:

(a) Gathering hard information.
(b) Gathering soft information from agencies dealing with that community.
(c) Gathering information from *personal contact* with members of that community.

It takes little effort to sit down and work out how to do this systematically. A simple brainstorming exercise usually produces a good list of sources of useful information. In addition, there are national agencies which provide information about particular communities of interest; Womens' Aid, the Commission for Racial Equality, Age Concern, Shelter, Mind, and so on. Contact with these agencies usually produces not only a wealth of relevant hard data, including legislation, and potential sources of funding, but also some information about how to set up particular projects, and the pitfalls thereof. More difficult to obtain, however, is statistical information for that community of interest, homeless people, drug users etc., which relates to a particular county or city, but local authority departments are also an obvious early port of call.

Getting into contact with ordinary members of a potential community of interest is often difficult because they are not linked by residence. Yet, if the approach taken is to be one of community development, whereby ordinary members of a community are being encouraged to organise to meet their needs, these are the people who have to be reached. Women suffering domestic violence, people with AIDS, unemployed people, drug users, for instance, may be contacted, in theory, through the agencies which purport to serve them. However, this is not always the best route to take, since many such people may not know about or be alienated from the

professional agencies. It is important to figure out
making these personal contacts.

Analysis, planning and organisation

A community profile is more than a collection of hard and soft
information. It is a tool upon which to build an analysis which
becomes the initial basis for action. When sufficient relevant
information has been obtained it has to be ordered,
emphasising not only the objective needs of the locality, but
also the more subjective perceptions of residents, in order to
identify opportunities for action. Unemployment may be an
enormous problem in the locality, for instance, but it may not
be possible to help residents organise to do anything about it.
If one or two residents have expressed the desire for a
parent-teacher association (PTA), a worker would need to
ask herself whether there would be much support from other
residents or from teachers for such an organisation, whether
becoming involved with a PTA would be in line with her
priorities and those of her agency, whether the necessary
resources were available, and so on. This way a worker builds
up some alternative possibilities for action. Each alternative
should ideally contain an assessment of its own advantages
and disadvantages, particularly the likelihood of sufficient
community support. Then it should be possible to make a
choice about which alternative or combination of alternatives
to select. The factors influencing one's decision about what to
get involved with are:

(a) one's own assessment of objective and subjective (hard
and soft) needs;
(b) what one's agency expects, and is geared up to do;
(c) one's own ideology or value system (what the worker
wants to do);
(d) the likelihood of success; and
(e) what people seem motivated to work on.

I also recommend that the advantages and disadvantages of
each possible action should be written on a piece of paper
using these five headings, in order to clarify which are the
most likely areas for productive action.

A worker should write down her community profile and

discuss it with her supervisor or consultant before proceeding to act upon it. However, community workers also proceed in a more opportunistic way. A couple of local people seem interested in an idea and, with the worker's help, are prepared to call a small meeting with friends to discuss it, and in no time at all a group gets off the ground. Of course community work happens like that, and it always will. That can be excellent practice. But it can also be bad practice, because if a worker is under external and internal pressure to get something done, she may be desperate to find an embryonic community group of any kind. She quickly becomes involved only to find later that the two residents who seemed keen to set up a group are fervently disliked by the rest of the community, or that she is spending all her working hours helping one group stay together while there are potentially more fruitful avenues to explore for which she no longer has the time. My objective in emphasising the analytical and planning skills is to prod potential community workers into devoting more attention to these than many of us do.

Conclusion

As community workers, our greatest asset is our enthusiasm; but it can also be our worst enemy. It is easy to get involved in a project because we want it to succeed rather than because it is likely to succeed. So we need to analyse carefully. On the other hand, too much analysis can cause paralysis. It is easy to argue why nothing will ever succeed. Good planning is also about risk-taking, but preferably calculated risk-taking. So it is not always wrong to embark on one course of action rather than another primarily because we want to, as long as we are aware that this is why we are doing it.

3

The Community Development Process II: Working with Community Groups

Introduction

A community development worker can do very little if the community members are not motivated. If they are she can do a great deal. However, bringing about change usually requires the power and legitimacy of an organisation. Thus, community development workers spend a good deal of their time helping members of particular communities to set up and run organisations. Such community organisations often form spontaneously, of course. But they sometimes die quickly when they are led by people with few resources or little relevant experience. It is the aim of the community development worker, operating within a value system which is ultimately to do with promoting social justice, to help those organisations to be more effective. That process is described in this chapter.

Intensive work to set up a group

For me the most important stages in setting up a community group are as follows:
(1)   contacting people and establishing an analysis of needs;
(2)   bringing people together, helping them identify specific needs and assisting them to develop the will to see that those needs are met;
(3)   helping them understand what will need to be done if those needs are to be met;

(4)   helping them identify objectives;

(5)   helping them form and maintain an organisation suitable for meeting those objectives;

(6)   helping them choose priorities, evaluate alternative lines of approach and design a plan of action, thus turning strategic objectives into a series of smaller objectives and tasks;

(7)   helping them divide these tasks between them and carry them out;

(8)   helping the members of the group feed back the results of their actions to the whole group which then has to evaluate those actions and adopt altered objectives;

(9)   stages 3 to 8 tend to become a permanent process which, after a time, becomes to some degree routinised, whereupon the worker may withdraw to a less intensive servicing role prior to withdrawing completely.

It needs to be noted however that while a generic neighbourhood worker can start with the open-ended brief suggested by this list a specialised community worker working with a community of interest often cannot. This is because she may be bringing only certain types of people together (homeless people, unemployed people or the parents of mentally handicapped people, for example) and so the general area of need is always clear. Also, the brief from her agency may well be fairly specific, to set up a centre for unemployed people, for example. For both these reasons the specialised community worker is often further along the road to deciding what is to be done before she comes into contact with the people from the community with which she is working. Thus she seeks to recruit people who have a potential commitment to a specific project, rather than trying to discover what it is they want.

Bringing people together

Let us now assume that a worker has worked out her analysis of the needs of the area and has some idea of her own objectives and the kinds of opportunities she is seeking. She may find that she spends some months making contacts without finding an issue or activity on which the community members seem prepared to take action. If that is the case, she will, at some point, have to consider whether there are any other ways to get a project going, by setting it up herself for example. On the other hand, she may find that a number of residents are concerned about the same problem, the poor bus service for example. At this point she will need to work out whether she might be prepared to help people organise to combat the problem. If her answer is positive she will take steps to sound the community members out a bit further. She may ask them, usually on an individual basis initially, if they had ever thought of trying to do something themselves about that need, whether there was anyone else they knew who felt the same, whether they would like to meet other like-minded people to see if anything could be done.

It is not too difficult to get people talking at the level of general needs, but the task of getting them to think about whether they might do something to alter the situation is more difficult. First of all it requires time. A worker who set up a successful women's group on an isolated housing estate spent many weeks visiting a large number of people in the area before moving ahead to set up the group. She visited some of the women five times, for example.

When a worker is trying to discover if people have the motivation to become involved, she has a mixture of tasks to undertake. She tries to identify points in the conversation when her 'contact' expresses a concern about community problems, such as the bus service. When this point is mentioned the worker may try to keep the conversation on this subject, probably by asking questions. 'What you said about the bus service – does anyone else feel the same?' Why do you think it is that the bus service is so poor?' 'Has anyone ever tried to do anything about it?' 'Have *you* ever thought of doing anything about it?' 'Would you be interested in meeting with a few neighbours to see if anything could be done about it?' It might only be through a process of several meetings that a subject was covered in that detail, but during these early stages of contact-making the worker's main objective will be to arouse the interest of people to take action. 'Hey, maybe there *is* something I could do after all', is the kind of feeling she wants to evoke. Then she has to help them to develop the *will* to act, which may take considerably longer.

At this stage, if she is a generic community worker, she may be able to respond positively to a range of ideas that people suggest. However, as she and some of the people with whom she is in contact begin to move towards an agreement to take action, her objective changes somewhat. From this point a worker is primarily trying to see how far other people are interested in that issue, although she may not have reached this stage unless she has already found several people who are in agreement about the general area of need. The next step is to bring them together. Often two or three keen people will meet to discuss the idea further. This may well happen without her suggesting it, and if so that is a good sign. They also need to understand it is *their* project. If possible the worker does not want to become seen as their leader. But in her enthusiasm to get the project moving the worker is likely to be seen in that way. Let us say that she is in contact with three women who have expressed interest in doing something about play. One way of moving ahead is to try to get them to arrange the first meeting between themselves rather than doing it herself. If they organise the first meeting this also tests their commitment and ability. Circumstances may dictate that the worker arranges the meeting, and many successful groups start that way, but it can be the slippery slope of worker over-involvement and the creation of dependence rather than autonomy in the people with whom she is working.

The people who are meeting together may already know each other, and that makes it easier for the worker in one way – but they may just chat. The worker needs to allow and encourage this informal interchange but at some point she must get them to focus on the needs which they are meeting to discuss. She can do this in many ways. For example, she can throw in ideas, ask questions, make statements, tell them what she thinks they should be doing or provide information. It may take several meetings to get them to focus on needs and objectives, and then they may find they are all interested in doing different things. Or, personality problems may emerge which make co-operation between them difficult. As a result they may not attend future meetings. It is important, however, to try to keep up the momentum. One way to do this is to make sure that a date is arranged for the next meeting, before which the worker meets the members individually yet again, and tries to plan with some of them what the meeting is to achieve. Conversely, if she has decided that she does not wish to continue with this group, a good way to let it die is to 'forget' to suggest a date for the next meeting!

With people who have not met each other before, different problems tend to arise; each individual may initially feel uneasy in the company of the others, for example. With such a group the worker may have to make considerable effort to break the ice. If she is shy or lacks confidence this can transmit itself to the group members, and she needs to give thought beforehand to how she can help them relax. Ensuring that a cup of tea is offered can sometimes help. It also helps to think about what casual subjects of conversation they are likely to respond to. The art of conversing casually in this way comes with practice and workers who are not naturally good at it must work at it. With a group of strangers there may be a 'testing out' period, and no real work will be done at the first meeting or so. It might take such a group longer to agree than it would a group of people who already knew each other.

Expanding the membership

Many groups start very small; two or three people perhaps, and gradually build up to six or seven. When there are very few members everyone should try to recruit more members. The worker, especially, should try to bring in more people because existing members will tend to recruit from their own contacts: friends, workmates, relations. Unless care is taken to recruit widely, community groups can become or become seen as cliques. Indeed they can often consist of members of the same family.

Personal contact is, again, the most important method of expanding the membership, but now there is something particular to 'sell' and the worker is wanting to recruit people with an interest in, for example, play. So, at this stage, other methods are also useful. Without calling a public meeting, which might be premature, it may be useful to give some wider publicity to the cause. The worker, or the group, may try to get an article in the press or on local radio, or it may be possible to get posters put in shops. However, not many people will come to a group where they know no one. Consequently, if a worker hears of people who might be interested, it is useful to call to see them, or to try to get a member of the embryonic group to do so. Personal contact works best.

Focusing on one objective

Let us say there are enough people for the group to start firming up on what it wants to do. A group tends to become a group and really start working out its objectives when it numbers five or six, and in many ways a group of about six is the ideal size. However, members often become despondent if they only get attendances of this number and the worker has to find ways of intimating that they are not doing too badly after all. At this stage the discontent or the desire to get something done is often unfocused and this leads straight to the first of a series of dilemmas. Should the worker allow the members to carry on in that unfocused way so that they become more comfortable with each other, and run the risk that those who are more task-oriented will leave? Or should she try to get them to focus on one area, and run the risk of pressurising them too much? It is a question of judgement and timing, and the only way of learning this is by getting it wrong a few times. It is useful for the worker to know her own predisposition, so that she can guard against it if necessary. Mine is to intervene too early. Therefore I have to force myself to wait. Others have more of a laissez-faire approach which may also need modifying on occasion.

Two problems may now become evident. First, some people who have never been involved in a project like this before may lack confidence. The problem will be to convince them they have the ability to do anything at all and to boost their morale. Second, people new to groups often want to achieve too much too quickly. For example, the group has agreed to focus on 'play' and one member says in early July, 'Let's run a summer play-scheme.' The rest agree and decide with enthusiasm that it should start next Monday and run every day for six weeks! When a group wants to jump straight into the action stage like this the worker has to find a way of helping them adopt realistic objectives such as, in this case a one-week play-scheme at the end of the holidays, or a more suitable time-scale in which it will be possible to undertake the necessary planning and organisation. Otherwise the worker may have to do a great deal of organising herself if the venture is to be successful.

At this stage the worker has to help the residents turn their discontent into a series of needs, the needs into a range of objectives and the objectives into tasks which are then allocated. She must also help them choose between different priorities. Would it be best to run a play-scheme or press the council to provide swings, for example? In evaluating these possibilities the question of resources also arises. How much money would be needed for a play-scheme and how would it be obtained? How many helpers would be needed and where would they come from? Who would recruit them? What are the time and skill implications of this for the group members? Whose permission would be needed if the group wanted to use the school playground and who will find out? A worker has to try to get the group to face questions like these in an informal way but it is their enthusiasm which keeps the group going at this point, and it is important not to extinguish that.

If possible the group must start with a success. To fail at the first attempt is likely to result in the death of the group. The secretary of a community group decided to hold a sponsored walk. I knew he was organising it badly and tried several times to encourage him to make better preparations. But he did not want to hear. It was an absolute disaster. Only a few children turned up and no one paid the money they collected to the group. Sometimes that is the only way to learn. But that community leader never ran another sponsored walk!

Directive democracy?

As it is usually practised in Britain paid community development work is largely a process whereby workers become involved in the natural process of the formation of community groups and assist them to become more effective. In some cases that natural process involves one or two group members (not the community worker) doing most of the organisational work, dominating the group, failing to ensure that new members are recruited, and, let me be frank, doing a poor job. Many community groups, especially pressure groups, fail, in my experience, to achieve their stated objectives and sometimes result in some group members being pretty badly served by their leaders.

The classic role of the community development worker is in a non-directive fashion to suggest ways in which the group can be a bit more effective and a bit less oppressive to those who are not its main leaders. This process works, but only to a degree. Therefore, I now think there is sometimes a case for a worker to take a role which is more directive, for the following reasons, Groups which are effective, both in terms of their instrumental goals and with regard to how they develop people, are difficult to create. A professional community development worker should know both the processes and the types of organisational arrangements necessary for achieving effective democratic collective action. Thus there is a good case for the worker, in certain situations to contract to work with an embryonic community group to help them structure themselves, to *train* them in how to organise themselves, and not to work with them on any other basis. Thus she becomes a kind of organisational consultant or trainer, just as an architect or a lawyer might advise a group on architectural or legal matters or even as a computer programmer might train people how to use computers, though the teaching style would need to be appropriate to the situation, to allow for discussion and so on. Here is an example.

An economic development funding agency agreed to provide £3000 to a community organisation for a study into the feasibility of establishing a community business. However, the money was only provided on the basis that the committee members agreed to undertake some of the feasibility work themselves and to work with the agency's consultant who would help them restructure their organisation so as to be more geared to running business activities.

As community organisations become more sop¹ and aim to run credit unions, manage their own hou.. estates or tender for community care contracts, for instance, the case for providing more formal training will become more evident. Today a number of support agencies will only work with groups which agree to undergo a particular training process. (See also pp. 65–6.)

Community workers have tended to play down their own expertise. But the expertise we have in building organisations is not common currency. Assuming we know our job, we ought, in some situations at least, to try to work only with groups whose members are prepared to put in the hard work necessary in order to learn the appropriate skills.

Organisational and interactional skills

Two rather different sets of skills are required in community work. The first of these are analytical, planning and organisational skills. If a group concerned with play decided to pressurise the local authority to provide conventional play equipment the worker should immediately begin to think of the practicalities. Where could the equipment be sited? Would it be vandalised? Would the council listen to a group of only six or is a public meeting or some other form of legitimation needed first? What other support would be necessary to convince the authorities, and what kind of evidence is needed to help the case? How should the case be presented? What kind of opposition should be expected? Where would political support come from? These strategical and tactical questions will lead on to organisational questions. What kind of organisation is needed to carry out this job? Do we need one person to write letters? Do we need to keep a record of decisions? Do we need a treasurer at this stage? What kind of mechanism should we have to ensure effective reporting back? How should we divide up tasks? Is headed notepaper necessary? What funds or person hours would be required? Who else has tried this and what can we learn from them? The group members will think of some of these points but there are likely to be gaps in their thinking. For instance, they may decide that a particular action will be taken but omit to decide who will do it, as a result of which it is not done. Our job is to advise on these organisational questions.

However, many people have analytical and organisational skills but would not make good community workers because they lack the ability to form relationships with other people in such a way that they will listen and take action on our advice. These are called interactional skills, and we use them, together with our organisational skills to help the group do its own analysis, planning and organisation. If we wish to communicate with other people we must be able to empathise with them while retaining a degree of detachment. We must not be so full of what we want to say that we do not see Fred and Joe exchanging angry looks or notice that Joan has been very quiet that evening. We need also to be aware of the background of the people with whom we are working because that helps us to understand what they are thinking and feeling. Then we are more likely to make appropriate rather than inappropriate comments.

Another important skill is saying clearly and simply what we mean and at an appropriate time. A common failing is the use of jargon; phrases like 'in-service training', or abbreviations unfamiliar to the audience. A related skill is learning to talk in parables, rather than in the language of ideas, and to use concrete rather than abstract words. We can train ourselves to become aware of the words we use and, if we get a colleague to tell us when she thinks we are not communicating, we can easily develop the habit of speaking in a simple way. But it needs working on.

The worker's role in meetings

During group meetings a community worker's job is to try to help the group move smoothly through the business. She may well have met with some members beforehand to plan the meetings, and they may be looking to her for support. She will be aware that new members, or other members who are not within the inner circle, have less knowledge than those who have prepared the meeting and she will want to make sure that they also understand and contribute to the proceedings. For most group meetings she will have thought about what

she wants to achieve. But her plan must be flexible and open
to alteration in the light of changing circumstances. When a
worker anticipates a difficult meeting it is useful to try to
predict what the difficulties will be and work out tactics to
deal with them.

Many different ways can be used to help a group learn to
make decisions. One good way is what Batten (1967) refers to
as the 'non-directive' approach. A main tactic within this
approach is to ask questions like: 'Didn't we decide last week
that we couldn't afford this?' 'Who did we decide would carry
that out?' The process of questioning can help people clarify
their own thoughts, which forms a necessary basis for action.
However, it does not always result in the group seeing the
point, let alone agreeing, and a more involved role is ofte
required, when the worker appears to be behaving more l`
one of the group, by making suggestions, arguing the cas'
a particular point of view, and so on. There may also be ti.
when the worker is quite sure the group is about to mak
mistake about which she wants to warn them firr
Obviously a worker must have a good relationship with
members if she is going to attempt this.

When using this 'non-directive' approach a worke
concerned to help the group members do things *their*
However, it is not necessary for her to conceal her own
or to pretend she has none. Indeed, if she does so, it is l
she will be perceived as vague and ineffectual. A great de
patience may also be necessary to allow the group membei
work problems out at their own pace. They may take ha`
hour to reach a decision the worker could have taken in t
minutes. A worker should also try to make clear the role
sees herself playing. If she has explained that her objectiv
to work only for a short time helping a group get off
ground and then to pull out, the people with whom sh
working have at least some chance of accepting or rejec
what is offered, and there is less danger of conflicts ari
from differing expectations about the worker's role. ´
understanding also helps us answer the charge that we
manipulating people, since our objectives are out in the oɪ

People new to groups tend not to think and act as part o
group when they are outside it. During the early meetings

group I was involved with, Marion used to turn up and say, 'I've run a bingo session in my house. Here's two pounds.' Although not previously sanctioned by the group, Marion's actions did no harm. But other independent actions can be disastrous. One of our tasks therefore is to teach the group members how to liaise with each other between meetings, to sound out ideas with each other, to plan together and to divide tasks between them.

Work with individual group members

If a group's key members can be helped to prepare adequately for a meeting, it is likely to be more successful. Thus a worker needs to spend time with those key individuals, helping them to work out agendas, implement decisions taken by the last meeting, and generally run the organisation as effectively as possible. Very often a member agrees in a meeting to perform a task which she has not fully thought through, and which may even be impossible. If the job is difficult she may well refuse to face the problem squarely and then make up a lame excuse at the next meeting for not having done it. Our task is to try to anticipate these difficulties and to help the group members overcome them. A member might have agreed to write to the housing manager on a particular issue. However, the worker knows that this member is not accustomed to writing letters of that nature, and should perhaps offer her help, but in such a way that it is not patronising.

People new to groups often talk a great deal about what they plan to do but do not get around to carrying it out. This happened with a local leader I was involved with. He was 'all talk' for some months. Then suddenly he started doing things; it was as if the talk was a preparation for the action.

Different group members have different ways of coping. Some put on a brave face and speak with assurance even when they are unsure. These members are sometimes very difficult to help because they feel too threatened to admit they need it. I often found myself colluding with such group members when they blamed other people for problems in the group for which they themselves were responsible. Any attempt by me to try to point out where their own actions had created the problem so often met with a denial, that I gave up trying to influence them directly and found other ways. When I wanted to influence one such community leader, I used to say to his wife something like: 'I've been wondering whether the group should try such and such. What would Ted think of this?' Sometimes this method worked, and Ted would approach me a month later and say 'Alan, I've had this great idea . . .

Other group members are too dependent; they rely too much on the worker and are reluctant to take responsibility themselves. To take the example of writing a letter to the housing manager, some people will always find ways of getting the worker to do it. In such a case ways must be found of getting them to do it themselves, such as by saying, 'This time I'll do it for you. But I'll show you how to do it and next time I would like you to do it yourself.' Again, if the worker has initially spelt out clearly how she sees her role – to create capacity in others, her task will be easier in such situations.

The leaders of community groups are sometimes in the job for highly personal reasons, to compensate for an unsatisfactory home or work life for example, although this does not necessarily affect the group. In general, however, there are not many good leaders of community groups, probably because running a community group is so difficult to do well, and there is one syndrome I wish to mention in particular. Some leaders do a great deal of work, but fail to delegate or even to consult the group. These leaders are often tolerated because of the work they do. But sometimes they go too far and the other members take them to task. At this stage the 'bad' leader can only cope by over-reacting, by becoming quite angry and by threatening to resign. Such people are also likely to feel threatened when new people join the group, particularly people with ability. They may also be suspicious of a community worker and perceive her as a threat. Yet these are the people we often have to work with and through.

Structuring the group

Dividing up or delegating tasks is difficult for most groups. This is because delegation requires thought about which tasks would be suitable, bearing in mind the abilities of the person who is to carry them out. If that person is not experienced her skills and confidence have to be built up slowly, which requires time and effort. This partly explains why the leaders of community groups almost always fail to train future leaders. In addition, those leaders who feel threatened by the existence of potential leaders often act, mostly unconsciously, in such a way as to discourage and exclude them. A worker, therefore, has a considerable task on her hands in getting the various leaders and potential leaders to work together.

There is also the knotty question of when or whether a group should be encouraged to take on a formal structure with officers and a constitution. People who are unused to committees should not be rushed into formal procedures. Whether a worker should try to get the group to formalise itself depends largely on what its objectives are. If it is mounting a campaign which needs careful co-ordination and planning, a clear delineation of roles and division of responsibility along the lines of a formal committee is necessary. But if the group is involved with activities which do not depend on good co-ordination in order to succeed, then it may not matter so much. Expressive groups, such as consciousness raising groups and social groups require much less formal organisation, for example, though care still needs to be taken that somebody notifies the members of meetings, books a room etc. But the device of a committee was invented to help a group of people take decisions in the most effective and democratic way. That is why formal organisations have constitutions and officers, and why they adopt procedures such as minutes, agendas, and so on. Whatever structure a group adopts, it must be geared to taking the kinds of decisions or actions which that group needs to take. If a worker is concerned that some members may be afraid of a formal committee structure but thinks that something is needed to stop meetings degenerating into unstructured chat sessions she must first discuss the matter with the members. She might start by suggesting that the group makes a list of the items for discussion at the beginning of the meeting and that someone keeps a record of decisions. Only later might she say that those were an agenda and minutes.

With the rotation of roles a similar problem arises, namely the tension between participation and effectiveness. In a group there may be one person who is quite good at chairing meetings, which is very difficult indeed to do well. Thus, the meeting may be better chaired if she does it for six months or a year. The problem is even bigger with the roles of secretary and treasurer where continuity is important. If a worker is concerned that the organisation should operate in this particular democratic way, namely, by rotating all major roles frequently, it is important to make sure that the structure adopted still enables the business to get done.

During the 1980s, partly as a result of the influence of the Women's Movement, non-hierarchical or collective organisation, as opposed to bureaucratic, hierarchical or top down organisation began to be emphasised. In some situations this can work, but it requires exceptional vigilance and co-operative attitudes, and may require a preparedness to spend midnight hours sorting out feelings and personal differences. Workers contemplating establishing this kind of organisation should do their homework and discuss the problems with others who have worked in collectives before they go ahead. (See Landry *et al.*, 1985 and Edwards, 1984, for some of the pitfalls involved in establishing collective and non-hierarchical forms of organisation.) My own view is that strictly non hierarchical groups are not effective at achieving complex instrumental tasks. On the other hand, all groups have to allow for consultation and influence both laterally and from the 'bottom' up. Also, on a much larger scale, organisations such as local authorities are increasingly seeking to find consultative and co-operative ways of operating and of relating these approaches appropriately to traditional line management. The issue is a major one for our society and a great deal of work still needs to be done to find ways in which organisations of all kinds can be democratic, effective and humane. (See, in particular Stanton, 1989, for both a thorough and a positive account of collective working.)

A related problem is that in any group of ten people or more, an 'inner core' tends to dominate. The rest may feel they are excluded from power. Therefore it is important to consider ways in which all members can be involved, at least in a small way. Then they will feel more involved and are less likely to drop out.

It is not generally appreciated that instrumental groups need 'engines'. 'Leader' is now an unfashionable word, but, whatever word is used, one person, as a minimum, has to ensure that the group's tasks are completed. If a group is not working, it is helpful to look to see if it has an engine or not.

Clarke covers in more detail many of the points I raise in this section in this handbook *Working on a Committee (1978)*. See also Pinder (1985) for a wealth of information about constitutions and other practical aspects of running groups.

The need for hard resources

The early writings about community development emphasised the relationship side of the work. Subsequently a greater emphasis was placed on the provision of 'hard' resources. These include printing facilities, a room to meet, information about housing legislation or how to give evidence at a public enquiry, as well as help from professionals such as lawyers and surveyors. Many facilities which seem small in themselves, such as the use of a telephone or typewriter, are vital for community groups, and if a worker can provide access to these she has a great advantage. A small amount of money for 'pump-priming' purposes is also useful. When a group is starting off it may need money for publicity or to book a room for a public meeting, for example. The provision of hard resources also helps convince people that the worker really is on their side.

To summarise, a worker who is helping a new group get off the ground will:
(a) attend group meetings in which her principal purpose will be to help the group take decisions;
(b) work with the members, mainly the leaders, by building their confidence and helping them plan meetings, for example;
(c) perform a number of tasks *for* the group such as discovering information.

In addition she may be recruiting new members and promoting the interests of the group in the various circles in which she moves.

Creating a constituency

No description of work to set up a community group would be complete if it did not give attention to the problem of establishing legitimacy and creating a constituency. When a group proposes to act on behalf of the community its members often consider it necessary to ensure a wide degree of community support by holding a public meeting. In practice, however, public meetings may be problematic. It is sometimes possible to hold a successful public meeting with no preparation, but one must be very sure of one's ground. Inadequate preparation can mean a poor turnout and despondency among the group members, an unruly meeting which the organisers canot control, or a meeting monopolised by one or two dominant individuals, councillors perhaps, which fails to achieve its objectives. There are also a number of other factors which cannot be controlled, the weather in particular.

A meeting must be well publicised, preferably in several different ways: by putting notices through doors and in shop windows, through announcements on local radio, by loudspeaker van, and most important, by word of mouth. A worker needs to use her imagination here. Sometimes schools will give children notices to take home, for instance. Then there is the question of organisation. Making arrangements like booking a room can be very time-consuming and cause problems, such as when you find the only room available is a primary school classroom with tiny chairs or that you cannot use the tea-making facilities. Considerations like the layout of the chairs are important. Most likely you will not want serried ranks of chairs but a semi-circle. That means someone must be on hand to organise it. It may also be useful to put out a few chairs initially, in case only a few people turn up.

The most important question is how to balance the democracy of a public meeting with control by the group. The group will go into the meeting with certain objectives – normally to get community backing to form an organisation with particular objectives and to recruit members. If possible one of the members of the existing group, which may still only number two or three at this stage, should chair the meeting.

But she will probably be reluctant to do this if she has not done so before. Also she might not be a very effective chair. If an inexperienced community member is going to chair it the worker may need to spend time helping her to prepare for various eventualities, how to cope with dominant councillors, for example. The worker also needs to think about the most appropriate role to take herself.

The next stage is more difficult – the election of the committee – which effectively is the basis of the organisation. It is imperative for the group to have some names of people in advance to put forward for the committee, especially for officers if there are to be any at this stage, because sometimes totally unsuitable people are nominated or there are no nominations at all. But, at the same time, the process should be seen to be democratic. If a meeting is seen as rigged, support may well vanish. One of my early meetings (not a public meeting) suffered from this problem. I had prepared with a very keen group member 'our' nominations for secretary, treasurer and chair. Instead of asking for nominations for each office, as a result of which everyone would have felt free to make suggestions, and during which process either of us could have suggested 'our' nominations, he took out the piece of paper on which I had written our nominations and said that these were the people he and I thought should take the offices, to my considerable embarrassment! Some key members never came again and shortly afterwards the group collapsed. I had failed to prepare this person adequately enough and had *assumed* that he would know how to handle the situation, but he did not. See Thomas (1976, pp.86-88) for further information on public meetings.

A common criticism of community groups is that they become out of touch cliques. Thus, it is important to try to help them retain their constituency. The best way of doing this is if the members have continuing personal contact with the rest of the community. A democratic device to ensure accountability, such as an annual meeting where the committee is re-elected and the actions of the group are open to scrutiny is often necessary too, but such meetings are not usually well attended. Another way is for the group to arrange representation according to streets. However, this requires a considerable degree of organisation, and it is rare for each street representative to report back to her constituency of neighbours once she has been elected, if elected she was. Other groups collect regular subscriptions or raise money through a door-to-door lottery. As both of these methods depend upon and renew personal contacts they require organisation and time. Public events such as exhibitions, jumble sales or summer fêtes, also publicise the group and arouse interest in the community.

A good method of publicising the activities of groups, thereby helping to create a constituency, is to run a regular newsletter. It is not too difficult to get the first issue together; but in doing this the group members realise how much work it takes and often the venture is dropped. It pays, initially, to keep a newsletter simple.

In an area where literacy skills are at a premium, people may not feel able to run a newsletter themselves. Shortly after I started work as a fieldworker, I asked residents whether a newsletter would be a good idea. They thought it was but did not say they would run it. I had the choice either to wait until they were ready or to run it myself. I chose the latter but made sure they wrote articles for it. Although many community workers pretend that local people run their own newsletter, it is often the community workers who do this. A newsletter may well be of high enough priority for a worker to consider doing it if local people cannot. But to produce one copy will take about a week's work. It also takes time for a newsletter to become well known, so magic results should not be expected. It should also come out regularly. Once every six months is better than six in the first year, three the next and then occasional issues at irregular intervals after that. See *Community Work through a Community Newspaper* (Armstrong *et al.*, 1976) and *Making News* (Lowndes, 1982) for a more detailed discussion of these questions.

Relationships with the outside world

Community groups often learn only slowly how to go about relating to the outside world in order to obtain what they want. Community workers ought to have knowledge of the workings of large organisations and will know, for example, that particular policies and procedures are laid down which cannot easily be bypassed, at least by community groups. Letters stay at the bottom of in-trays and 'progress chasing' is necessary to make sure answers are received. People new to community action often know none of this (though they know many other things better than community workers) and do not always appreciate the need to follow particular procedures. I remember several meetings when I felt like a killjoy, explaining to a group, for example, why it would be very difficult to overturn the policy that a Parks Department football pitch could not be hired on a Sunday. On the one hand it is often better to explain these formalities, in order to prepare people for the response they will probably get if they tackle the outside world in the 'wrong' way, rather than allowing them to go ahead and come back defeated. On the other hand, there is no substitute for people learning through direct experience that the way they want to do something will not work and that other avenues must be explored. The way to do this productively is to try to create situations where the group will learn in a real way not just that a particular approach will not work, but why, and how to circumvent the problem. In the above example it might have been a good idea to get the Parks Superintendent and the chair of the Parks committee to a meeting to explain the policy to the group, rather than doing it myself.

Not surprisingly community groups are often very unsophisticated at first and may deal with the authorities inappropriately, sometimes with simple aggression, which does not usually produce the required results, and alienates councillors. Over time, however, most groups can be helped to become more sophisticated, so that they learn to negotiate effectively with other power-holders.

Professionals in groups

When a community group contains professionals such as youth workers or teachers, co-operation can be difficult, since the culture and reference points of 'community' people and 'professionals' may be very different. On the other hand, the exchange which these groups can create is sometimes very productive. Residents learn from professionals the problems of operating a home-help service, for example; and professionals learn from residents, in an immediate way, how people feel about community needs. However, professionals often take a leadership rather than an enabling role, dominate the residents and impose their own agendas. If this happens and the professional does not respond to tactful hints the worker may have to have a word with her outside the group. Sometimes groups discipline dominant members themselves, but this is difficult with high-status outsiders.

Work with existing groups

If a worker is asked to become involved in an existing group or she takes the initiative to contact it she may operate rather differently from the way in which she would work with a group which she started. She may have been asked by the existing group for specific advice, on how to draw up a constitution or to apply for a grant, for instance. Similarly, a worker may have made contact with an existing group because she wants to assist it to become more effective or because she has other tasks in mind which she thinks it could take on. I once contacted a community association on a neighbouring estate which purported also to cover the estate on which I worked. My objective was to make that association more aware of needs on 'our' estate and to open it up to representatives of community groups from our area. I succeeded in getting members of organisations on our estate elected but they soon became disillusioned with the existing members' lack of concern about our estate, and left.

group to that end. Similarly, it is much easier to help a group develop and strengthen its work in an area in which its members are already interested, than to get them to change their focus.

Where a group has asked a worker to help with a specific problem, it is relatively easy for her to say she is prepared to do A, B or C, but not X, Y and Z; that is, to establish an explicit agreement about what she is prepared to offer over an agreed time scale. It should be our objective to arrive at this degree of explicitness with all groups with which we work, but it is more difficult when we set up new groups because the members will not normally be ready, at least initially, for a clear statement of our aims and objectives. We have to convey these more subtly. It is also sometimes the case that our relationship with groups which came into existence without our help is not so intimate as with those which we helped to create. (See also pp. 65–6.)

Reviving moribund groups

When I wanted to revive a particular group, I came across a problem which in various forms is familiar to many community workers. The association existed in name only, and the secretary was the only member! This person was still committed to the association and it seemed appropriate to work with him to re-establish it. However, he was not popular in the area and his presence might have prevented other people from joining. I was concerned about him as a person and his feelings if I made no effort to involve him, so I partly involved him by telling him about meetings but doing most of the work with other individuals. However, I felt uneasy working in this way, probably because I had not fully made up my own mind what to do. In this kind of situation it is important for the worker to think carefully about priorities and the extent to which she is prepared to continue working with such individuals.

When a group was declining I sometimes asked the members whether it should be disbanded. This normally resulted in people deciding to carry on, perhaps because they would not face the fact that they failed. In retrospect, I now believe that I should not merely have asked the members this question, I should have thought about it deeply myself and have tried to get them to explore the question seriously, rather than dealing with the issue only at a superficial level.

It would be unethical to work behind the scenes to destroy a group, but if a worker comes to believe that a group should disband I think she should find the right time and then state that, in her view, the group should cease to exist, and explain why, but also listen to arguments why it should not. She would then either withdraw or work with the agreement of the existing members to help it wind up. I think it is important to try not to collude but to engage with people on real issues, though this can be very difficult.

A directive approach to setting up a group

Community workers are paid to improve the quality of life for a community largely by assisting the development of community groups. But what happens if, after six months' or a year's work, this proves impossible? Two workers tried to help gypsy families on an unofficial site organise in order to put their case to the authorities for the provision of basic facilities, such as refuse collection, and to press for an official site. No organisation emerged after two years' work.

When no group emerges after considerable work one option is for the worker to set something up herself. With regard to the gypsy site, workers came to the conclusion that as group organisation was an alien method of approach for the gypsies, they, the workers, should become involved in setting up other activities, such as a literacy scheme and a summer play-scheme. The objective was to show the gypsies that something positive could be done, and thereby to engender within them the idea that they could act for themselves. As long as it is sensitively done, playing this kind of leadership role can enhance the capability of people in the community to take action themselves, rather than inhibit it. But it should not be confused with initiating projects without reference to community groups, which is covered in chapter five.

However, if our ultimate objective is that community members should run schemes themselves there is no guarantee that they will ever take them over if the worker runs them initially. Also, it is easy to deceive ourselves when acting as a leader that it is really the people who are running the scheme, that they are leading and we are advising, whereas in reality they see us as the leader. When I tried to set up an anti-motorway action group, which local people certainly wanted, I initially made this mistake. I gathered people together and we started various actions, raising money in particular. Only when I discovered that I was doing all the work did I realise that although I saw the group as theirs, they saw it as mine! They would follow if I led, but they would not lead. I later accepted this and led because 'product' in this situation was more important than 'process'.

Work with larger organisations

An organisation is needed for community action to take place. But the tasks community groups take on often require a more sophisticated and powerful organisation than most disadvantaged communities are capable of creating. In many situations this results in the job still getting done but less successfully. The carnival is badly organised but still takes place, for example. In other situations poor organisation is a recipe for total disaster.

The example of the creation of a community association will illustrate the problems and needs of larger organisations. Community associations are 'umbrella' organisations which bring together representatives from existing groups and sometimes statutory bodies, as well as representatives direct from the neighbourhood. Their purpose is to take up or promote a range of issues or activities and these often include the management of a community centre. If a community association is to be set up the following questions need considering. Which groups and organisations should be asked to send a representative to the governing body? Do you want political parties? Do you want councillors? Do you want shopkeepers and industry? If so, should they have a vote? Do you want representatives from pubs, working-men's clubs, the trades council? What kind of representation should the local authority departments have, if any? What about the status of professional workers in the area such as youth workers, clergy? Should individuals be allowed to join the governing body (let us call it a council)? If the council is to be truly representative it will be quite large: thirty people at least. How often should it meet? Should you really try to run everything through this council or should there be sub-committees: to run the newsletter, the carnival, the play-schemes, or to fight the motorway proposal? How will such sub-committees differ in practice from similar but independent community groups constituting the organisation? How will their work be co-ordinated? Can the council co-ordinate them or is a smaller executive committee necessary which meets more frequently? If the council only meets every two months, how can important decisions be taken qucikly? If there is an executive committee how can it make sure that the council members do not feel they are just rubber-stamping decisions already taken? How will financial control be managed? Will the table tennis group have to get permission from the council to buy new table tennis balls? Should sub-committees spend the funds they raise or must they pay some or all to the central organisation?

Who is to take the minutes and type, duplicate and distribute them? What resources will be needed to ensure that the various parts of the organisation communicate with each other? Do they need equipment of their own, a duplicator or a minibus, for example, and if so how will these resources be managed? Is the organisation so big that it needs to employ paid staff, a part-time secretary for example. If so, how will he or she be managed? What finance will be needed and how should this be obtained? Is it necessary to register as a charity? Should there be individual subscriptions and if so, how should these be collected? How do you get 'ordinary' people to participate in an organisation which has had to develop formal procedures in order to manage itself? How do you prevent it being seen by ordinary people as 'them' rather than us?

In large community organisations five or six people, possibly fewer, will run the organisation between them. In theory, decisions are democratic. In reality they are taken outside the formal meetings by one or two people who often do much of the work implied by the questions in the previous paragraphs. Making a large community organisation function properly on an entirely voluntary basis in an area where there does not exist a great deal of organisational expertise requires, in my view the services of a community worker. Although it is sometimes possible for the worker to withdraw from 'primary' community groups, it is often not possible to withdraw from a more complex, multi-purpose organisation.

These are just some of the organisational considerations to which we must give attention when trying to establish complex organisations. But there are also the interactional tasks. Whatever our ideas are as community workers, we have to take the various 'actors' with us. In the end, we have to help them establish the organisation they want and they, in turn, require interactional skills in order to involve their own members.

Larger organisations have potentially more power than simpler one-purpose organisations. In practice this is not always the case, particularly with umbrella organisations composed of people representing a range of interests: scouts, youth club, tenants' association, old people's group, head-teacher, social services, and so on. Such an organisation will tend to move at the pace of the slowest or the most conservative and it is much easier to prevent action being taken than to initiate it. Umbrella organisations which consist of the same type of constituent group, where there is considerable agreement both about the problems and the means with which to solve them, such as federations of tenants' associations, are on occasion able to muster a considerable amount of power. However, even then one narrow interest group can still dominate. In Swansea a federation of tenants' associations was once established. But its key member associations concentrated on the problems of certain houses made of steel which were now corroding. The other constituent associations whose members lived in brick-built houses eventually left. Consequently if we are involved in setting up an umbrella organisation which we want to become a powerful agent for change, we need to think carefully both about which groups are represented and how to keep all groups involved.

The large community organisation has a tendency to become remote from its constituency and therefore out of touch with needs. It can also act as a buffer between 'primary' community groups and the local authority which may expect these always to go through the umbrella organisation. The other major problem is that it is difficult for a member of an umbrella organisation to be loyal both to her primary community group (and of course she may be involved in several of these) and to the umbrella organisation. This increases the likelihood that the umbrella organisation will be dominated by a small clique which is not in touch with the needs of 'primary' community groups. It requires vast amounts of community work time to ensure the links are kept between these constituent groups and the centre.

If a worker is working with a complex community organisation she may find that her relationship with it resembles that of a local authority chief officer to her committee: she will find herself acting rather like the employee of the organisation. She also needs to think about whether she should attend the organisation as a member, which she may be eligible to do. It is, however, difficult to play the enabler role at the same time as one is acting as a member, particularly if one also has the job of secretary or any other office. If one is the secretary of a large organisation there are so many executive tasks to undertake which involve heart as well as head, and where actions taken must sometimes be argued for and defended, that it is often impossible to stand back and consider the organisational questions necessary for the maintenance and future development of the organisation. (See Taylor *et al.* (1976), Salmon (1974), Lees and Mayo (1984), North Tyneside CDP (1978) and Henderson and Thomas (1981) for more information on work with federations and Twelvetrees (1976 and 1985) for an analysis of community associations.)

Withdrawal

A common catchphrase is that a community worker's job is to make herself redundant, but this can be misleading. Certainly a worker can and should withdraw from particular activities or situations, but often there will be other needs requiring her attention within the same area of work. In the long term she may be able to say that a particular community can take care of its own needs and turn her attention to areas of greater need. But as far as deprived, poor, or oppressed communities are concerned the process is very long indeed. For instance self-advocacy groups of persons with a mental handicap mostly have facilitators (who are a kind of specialist community worker), but these facilitators usually service the self-advocacy groups on a permanent basis.

It is possible to identify three types of withdrawal, which are not necessarily sequential. These are:

(a) withdrawal from an intensive role to a servicing role;
(b) withdrawal from a servicing role;
(c) leaving one's job altogether.

However, the principles of withdrawal are very similar for each type.

Withdrawal is often handled badly; partly, perhaps, because of the emotional implications. It is likely that the worker gets some satisfaction from being in the centre of the action. She may not cope easily with the loss of status which is normally implied by no longer being centrally involved with a project. She may feel lost if a group is no longer dependent on her.

There are likely to be many different forces which influence a worker's decision to withdraw; not only demands on her time from other areas of work but also her own feelings of frustration with a particular group. The feelings created of guilt, or of no longer having a purpose, are uncomfortable and it is often easier not to face them. But only if they are faced can one deal with them and withdraw in such a way as to benefit the group. The emotions of the group's members also need to be taken into account.

It takes time to withdraw well, because, in the early stages, not only is a worker carrying out her old role of servicing the group, but she is also probably training a group member or searching out another professional to take over certain of her functions. Furthermore, it takes a great effort to devote extra attention to the group when one has already left it behind mentally and is reaching out to pastures new. It is during withdrawal, above all, that one's policy of being as open as possible with the group will pay off. If a worker has initially given the impression that she will be around for ever and that she is like any other member of the group, she should not be surprised if the members are angry and upset when she tells them she is leaving next week and if her successor in the job tells her that this group will have nothing to do with him. However, it will be easier if she has initially emphasised that her job is only to help establish the group and then to move out, and if she discusses her changing role with the group from time to time.

There is also the question of whether and when to withdraw. The first consideration should always be whether the group will decline or collapse without the worker. This is difficult to judge and is complicated by the fact that any worker reaches a point of diminishing returns. The initial period of intensive work, if successful, sees a marked development in the effectiveness of the group. But, even if a worker continues to work intensively, the rate of improvement tends to slow down. She then needs to consider what to do. It is likely, however, that her aspirations are for the group to achieve a higher level of functioning than is actually possible. When the group's performance begins to level off she has the choice of either continuing to work intensively or withdrawing to a servicing role. If she withdraws to a servicing role there are two main scenarios. First, the group might continue in existence at the same or a slightly lower level of functioning. Second, it could decline to nothing, either slowly or quickly. In deciding whether to withdraw, either completely or from an intensive role to a servicing role, a worker needs to work out which of these or other scenarios is the most likely and plan her action accordingly.

No action is taken in isolation. When a worker is considering withdrawal it is normally within the context of other claims on her time. There will be other groups or projects with which she may be involved. Perhaps a group is starting somewhere else to which she could be of use, but she knows that she does not have the time to work with this group as well as other groups. Certain kinds of groups will also have greater priority for her than others. If she has spent a considerable amount of effort setting up a mechanism whereby tenants' representatives meet regularly with housing officials, she will probably be very unwilling to risk the death of the groups which form the constituency for those representatives. Consequently she might never withdraw from work with such groups.

However, it is salutary to remember that it is natural for a community group to spring up for a particular purpose and then to decline and die. It is possible that the desire among community workers to preserve groups at any cost may inhibit the formation of other groups. Alternatively, if one allows this natural process of birth, development, decline and death to take its course, the groups with which one works may never reach the stage of dealing with complex matters or negotiating effectively with major power holders. A worker must decide whether the continuation of a particular group is likely to play a part in her future strategy, in which case she will probably continue to service it in the long term. However, a worker often has to withdraw before the group can stand on its own feet, and there will be nobody who can continue her work to support it. In that case she should help the group establish contact with a range of individuals who can offer help in specific areas. She should also try to link the group with other groups which have similar objectives, the members of which can sometimes offer advice and help.

Inevitably the stages of withdrawal from intensive work through routine servicing to complete withdrawal tend to merge. When a worker is servicing rather than working intensively with a group, she may attend some or even all group meetings. She may also provide limited services on an agreed basis. It is possible that she will have contact outside the group with some group members. But the group is less dependent on her. The onus of responsibility for her involvement has begun to shift from her to the group and she needs to ensure that the group members appreciate this. It is now more up to the group to ask her for help or advice. She becomes less a teacher, more a consultant, reactive rather than 'pro-active'.

Once a worker has withdrawn to a routine servicing role she should be wary of becoming involved intensively again. My experience was that quite often a crisis would arise in a group just after I had withdrawn and I would feel a great moral pressure to take up my old role. Unless a worker withstands that pressure she may never succeed in withdrawing. When withdrawing she must also find ways of demonstrating that she still regards the work the group is doing as important because, whatever people say, they may still feel emotionally that she is betraying them.

When she withdraws completely, and is no longer involved even in routine servicing, a worker will probably wish to maintain a minimum of contact; perhaps by issuing an invitation to contact her in the future if the members think she could be of use. She might also make an effort to attend the annual general meeting, or occasionally call on the chair to hear how the group is getting on.

When a worker leaves her job the process of withdrawal is rather different. Within one month she may have to withdraw totally from a group with which she has been working intensively, and that is difficult to do well. Ideally, as is mentioned above, we need to inform the people with whom we are working that we are thinking of moving on so as to give them a chance to consider the implications. Then, when we have obtained another job we should give ourselves plenty of time to withdraw decently. I found three months adequate.

To conclude: the process of withdrawal is as critical as the initial stages of establishing the group. In a sense it begins the day we start.

Contract work?

The previous section emphasises the importance of the worker clarifying with the group how she perceives the situation and also indicating clearly what she can and cannot offer. Ideally, community groups should be able to engage community workers as consultants in order to help them achieve particular objectives, as they might hire a lawyer or an architect. As community work becomes more established and community groups adopt sophisticated goals this method of working may develop. In the USA it is often now the case, for instance, that a community organisation will hire a support agency to undertake a piece of work – training perhaps – and the support agency will assist the community organisation to obtain a grant which is then paid to the agency for the work. This kind of relationship between a community organisation and a support worker or agency is potentially very important, since it enables the dignity of the members of the group to be maintained in that they know what they are getting, and can control it, rather than being under the control of the worker.

Using the media

It is sometimes important for groups to get publicity in order to boost the confidence of the members, to attract new members or to mobilise support in a campaign. Unfortunately, local newspapers, in particular, often misinterpret information. Even if a reporter has been invited to an event, she may not attend. Or she may highlight a minor remark, making it seem as if the group is criticising the council when it is not. Reporters also often try to talk to people who they consider will be articulate, such as community workers, but they can gradually be 'trained' to talk to 'community people'. However, if group members are going to talk to the press they need briefing beforehand to ensure that the correct story is printed. For example, the chair of a parent-teacher association who was interviewed on the day of a well-attended fête, criticised the community for lack of support, and his words appeared as a headline the next day.

We cannot control the press. But we can control the information we give them, and it is useful to have a short press release prepared. Or we may decide to dispense with a reporter and merely take our own press release plus a photograph into the office. However, a story has to be presented in such a way as to be newsworthy. It pays also to establish good contact with the news editor of the local paper, who can advise how to get the best coverage.

With local radio the problems lie in being adequately prepared for a variety of questions and in giving local people the confidence to use this medium. People become used to speaking on the radio fairly quickly and when they have been on the air once they are usually prepared to do so again. They may need support or encouragement to start with however. See 'How to cope with the media' (Rote, 1979) and *Voluntary Organisations and the Media* (Jones, 1984), for some practical hints in this respect. There are now also training courses on public speaking and media presentation which can sometimes be helpful.

Managing money

Allegations of financial mismanagement cause enormous antagonism within community groups. While the financial affairs of community groups are ultimately their own concern, community workers have a responsibility to ensure that the members are aware of the problems they will have to deal with. We may not know how to keep basic accounts and so we might not be too bothered if we find out that the treasurer is keeping a note of everything on the back of a cigarette packet! But we would be worried if we discovered that the books did not balance and the rest of the committee was accusing her of embezzlement! After initially adopting a laissez-faire attitude to book-keeping, I gradually became firmer, especially when activities involving substantial amounts of cash were taking place on premises for which I was responsible. It is vital that treasurers should know how to keep proper accounts before things go wrong, as it is then often too late to rectify the situation. Community workers and local treasurers will find *Basic Book-keeping for Community Groups* (Jim Smith, 1979) very useful. (See also, Pinder, 1985, pp. 61-80). Or get a private accountant's advice.

The law

The law impinges on community work in many ways, from the need to obtain planning permission for a change of building use to the laws relating to demonstrations. It is often easy to embark on a project without considering the legal implications, which results in enormous complications when such regulations impinge on the enterprise. Thus, it pays always to consider the legal implications of any project in advance.

Relationships with politicians

A friendly councillor can sometimes be a great help to a community group, while an unsympathetic councillor can be enormously obstructive. However, a majority of councillors need to vote at the council meeting in order to bring about a change in policy or procedure and to allocate resources (even though the decision may have been taken, in effect, beforehand). Therefore a community group must be able to convince significant councillors, that the decision should go in its favour. Notwithstanding the low poll at elections, most local politicians see themselves as being elected to make decisions for the whole electorate. Consequently many are rather suspicious of community organisations which have no similar mandate or responsibility. They will often see the community worker as a threat because she is involved in activity which may challenge them, and so they sometimes over-react to pressure. Of course we are sometimes involved in disagreements and battles with councillors, but care must be taken not to alienate them unnecessarily.

Close contact between community groups, community workers and councillors can help the latter to understand the needs, problems and perspectives of people at local level and therefore, to argue their case better in committee, but any councillor will have other pressures from officers, from her party, and from central government. Consequently, she will not always be able to represent the interests of the community group favourably in the council. There is a particular danger here with a friendly councillor. If she gives help to a group its members may become dependent and too readily accept the situation when she says that nothing can be done. The group should still make its own representations to the council rather than relying entirely on the councillor. Workers also need to ensure as far as possible that the councillor is not part of the community group but attends meetings, or parts of meetings, clearly in her councillor role. This is not always easy, particularly if she is also a member of the community.

Members of Parliament are inevitably more remote than councillors, but they can sometimes intervene with effect in more local matters. A letter from an MP to the leader of the council, particularly if it draws attention to a procedure which was not properly followed, can sometimes ensure that a case is re-examined, for instance.

The question of relationships with politicians raises the further question of how far we should allow our own party political affiliation, if we have one, to be evident in our professional work. Two over-simplified views are as follows. Many workers contend that as community work is about furthering the interests of working-class and oppressed people, it inevitably means a party political struggle; we are partisan and should not hide it. My view is that if community groups become *perceived* as pursuing narrow party political goals, and if workers become *perceived* as being party agents in disguise either by our managers or by elected representatives, we are likely to receive far less co-operation from council officials and from councillors in general, not merely from those in opposing parties, and will find it more difficult to obtain our objectives.

Living in the area

To be an effective neighbourhood community worker, should one live in the area in which one works? This question is complex and requires careful consideration in each individual case. The geographical areas in which community workers operate differ in size and homogeneity. If a worker is working across one district within a county it may be convenient, possible and desirable to live in the area without this creating too many problems. Also, living in a small, one-class housing estate can have its advantages. The worker makes contacts easily. She identifies strongly with the needs of other residents, who also identify with her because, to a degree, she is one of them. However, the disadvantage is that whenever she is at home or going about her personal business in the area, she is likely to be 'at work'. Consequently, she may not be able to relax. There is also the danger of losing the degree of objectivity which is necessary for good practice. The worker becomes so involved with the day-to-day work she never stands back and reflects upon it. The benefits of living in the area can be great; but so is the price we pay. Therefore, workers should do whatever they feel able to do. They should not feel guilty about not living in the area if they think they can survive better by living outside it.

An even more demanding form of living in the area is living on the job. When I was a fieldworker I lived with my wife (who was not employed as a community worker) in a council house which served also as office, advice centre, and meeting place for groups. In this situation a worker can feel guilty if he is upstairs watching television and a group is meeting downstairs without him. What does he do when he is ill? People call at all hours, often on trivial matters, and this can be difficult to tolerate for long. The pressures on a partner can also be considerable.

The paradox of buildings

Community groups need places to meet, but their members need to be made aware of the time and effort required to manage a community building. In particular, the members have to consider ways of running the building without sacrificing other activities. One way is to form a separate organisation to run it if there are sufficient members to make this practical. See *Community Associations and Centres* (Twelvetrees, 1976) for a detailed discussion of these questions. If the worker has responsibility for managing even a small building, this may take her a minimum of a day per week: cleaning and caretaking must be arranged, wages paid, and a booking schedule organised. If the building is used for multiple purposes, for example as an advice centre, meeting place and as office accommodation, there will be conflict between the various interests. If a disturbance is caused neighbours may have to be placated. The creation of a user committee can sometimes help, and often many of these tasks can be delegated to a caretaker. But it still takes some time to liaise with the user groups and to manage the caretaker.

Some community buildings have bars, and this area can be a minefield. (See *Licensing and other statutory requirements* NFCO (n.d.) for guidance.)

Community groups and self-funding

In the current ethos in Britain community groups are sometimes expected to become self funding, particularly if they have a resource such as a community building. These aims are, in every case I have met, unrealistic. However, with a proper business orientation, which need not be in conflict with philanthropic goals, a group with a resource of that kind could raise a greater proportion of its running costs, say 50 per cent rather than 10 per cent. There is a strong case for ways to be found of helping groups acquire this expertise, primarily through training and consultancy.

Community business?

From the late 1970s community groups began to seek ways of creating employment, often using central government job creation or youth training funds. As such monies have become less available community groups and community workers have tried to set up community businesses which create 'real' jobs for the members of disadvantaged communities. The evidence suggests that people who might not otherwise have found a job or set up their own business can sometimes be helped to do so. But there is always a high fall out rate even though the people who do not go on to run a business may still have benefited considerably. In fact, many projects, for example CREATE in Cleveland (England) focus on encouraging people to be enterprising in the belief that the benefits of enterprise will feed through to jobs in the long run but also because there are many other benefits. The evidence about how far community groups are able to establish successful businesses suggests that this is extraordinarily difficult to do, creates few jobs, does not create a surplus for community activities, and may even require a continuing subsidy if it is to be successful. If a worker is concerned to help a group run a community business she needs to do a great deal of homework first and to learn about the criteria for success in business, which are well known. For instance, effective business requires good management, business plans, appropriate marketing techniques, adequate capitalisation and a skilled workforce. It also needs to make a profit unless it is to go under. The particular danger with community-led enterprises is that social goals can be confused with economic goals. An instance of this would be to employ people who needed jobs rather than people with the skills to do the particular jobs, as a result of which the product would be of inferior quality, which can lead to bankruptcy. Employing people who need jobs rather than people with appropriate skills is not a problem if the loss in profit can be made up in another way, by grants or by a considerable amount of voluntary work, upon which some community businesses survive. But these kinds of support are not usually there for long. See Willmott (1989) for an excellent, brief, but somewhat pessimistic summing up of community business in the UK, and Twelvetrees (1989) for a description of the USA experience in this respect.

Advice centres

Some new workers think that a good way to initiate community involvement is to set up an advice centre. The implicit assumptions of a worker who is doing this are often first, that residents will run the service, and second, that individual advice work will generate collective action. But these things do not always happen. When setting up an advice centre the worker is not acting as an enabler but as an initiator. She will also need to be in the building during opening hours which must be closely adhered to if she is to establish any credibility. Consequently she cannot be working outside the building at the same time. Advice and information work is a semi-profession in its own right, and for every hour the centre is open she will have to spend at least another hour collecting and organising information, keeping up to date on legislation, and taking further action on some of the individual issues which come up. This will all detract from work with community groups, although, if the advice work is resourced properly it can also link in with other work by bringing the worker into contact with more people.

There are also other points to consider. For example, how does a worker generate a free and easy atmosphere, involve residents in helping each other and at the same time preserve confidentiality? Some centres are 'drop in' centres where people are encouraged to do just that, and to stay as long as they like. This approach can be excellent but it also has disadvantages. Some people may become upset because they feel that certain individuals or groups are monopolising the place, for example. The worker also runs the danger of losing sight of her objectives. She may feel she is doing useful work just because she is in contact with people all day, without ever working out what she is trying to achieve (mindless activism!) Nevertheless, advice and information play an important part in many community projects, and represent one of the successful innovations which have resulted from community work. See *Community Action* (No. 30) for information on how to set up an advice centre, and Astin (1979) and Jerry Smith (1979) for two thoughtful accounts of some of the problems mentioned here.

Work with communities of interest

The main principles of work with locality based groups apply also to work with communities of interest; 'starting where people are', identifying self interest, establishing relationships through personal contact, the steps which it is necessary to take in building an organisation and so on. However, there are also some major differences. The first difference is that it is much more difficult to reach the ordinary members of those communities. People with Parkinsons' disease or women suffering domestic violence often have to be contacted via the professionals who work with them. Second, people who live in the same neighbourhood are more likely to know each other and to meet in pubs, launderettes, on the way to work, outside the primary school and so on. If one of them misses a meeting the local grapevine will let them know what happened and the date of the next one. They will be served by the same district and county councillors, may well use the same doctor and will have many other natural linkages with each other. More importantly perhaps they may be of a similar class and culture and share many of the same needs because of the nature of the areas where they live – poor transport, inadequate public housing, pollution from nearby factories, the lack of playspace, for instance. The members of 'communities of interest' usually share none of these advantages with regard to the formation of community groups. Moreover, the particular characteristics they share – alcoholism for instance – may be the only thing they have in common. Thus, the membership of a community group based on a community of interest is likely to be much more heterogeneous and, for this and the other reasons mentioned, more difficult to organise.

Rural community work

Most of the writing about community work in Britian is based on an urban model. There are, however differences between urban and rural work. For instance the difficulty of people getting to meetings means that more work is done with individuals outside group meetings than is done in urban situations. (See Francis and Henderson, forthcoming, for an introduction to rural community work.)

Community social work

The phrase 'community social work' was coined by the Barclay Report (1982) which suggested that social workers should work in indirect ways as well as direct ways to help clients, and as social care planners rather than merely as counsellors. Since then there has been a plethora of books, articles and projects which have explored these ideas.

Community social work is particularly associated with decentralised forms of organisation – often called patch social work – where social workers operate in very small teams in neighbourhoods (See Hadley and McGrath, 1980; and Hadley *et al.*, 1987). However, in my view the essence of community social work is a value system concerned with enabling, empowering and involving the community, facilitating the growth of mutual aid, modifying or changing the system, team work, co-operation between different departments and the breakdown of unnecessary professional distance. (See Hadley *et al.*, 1987, p. 11). In many respects the patch type of organisation may be most appropriate to deliver services which are consistent with these values, but this would not necessarily always be the case. See also Baldock (1974) and Pinker's appendix to the Barclay Report (1982), for two different critiques of the patch idea.

To start with therefore, any worker contemplating becoming a community social worker should try to be clear about objectives. However, a community social work approach has to be department wide. It is virtually impossible to sustain on any other basis. Moreover, managers need training in it as well as field staff, since it requires a much more consultative form of management, both vertically within departments and laterally to other organisations.

An individual worker also needs to be clear whether she is a community social worker or a specialised community worker. Simply put, a community social worker uses approaches and attitudes central to the philosophy of community work to help her clients more effectively. She does this in a variety of ways, but an important one is to get to know the community she works in so that she can, for instance, involve the local Age Concern group in supporting a lonely elderly person. On the other hand, a community worker specialising in social service work would be aiming to strengthen coping networks in a community in order to ensure that people at risk were better cared for. The difference is that the community social worker's main concern would be for the immediate wellbeing of her clients while the specialised community worker's concern would be to develop new or modified organisational arrangements to ensure that better services were provided, and which in addition, involved consumers in determining those services as much as possible. Thus, the specialised community worker would have to neglect individual clients if she was to do her main job properly. A constant complaint made by social workers who are trying to work closely with the community is that when an individual client needs a great deal of attention, the worker is forced to stop her other work.

During the 1970s many attempts were made by social workers to develop new forms of work and to add a community dimension to social work, but for every success there were many failures. One problem lay in the relationship between community work and social work. Social workers were encouraged to think that they could now do community work too, but there were not enough people with experience of community work in senior positions or teaching it to illuminate the pitfalls. There were also other problems, such as the growing volume of central government legislation, which a social worker had to understand and implement without the necessary resources. This process is continuing today with, in addition, new areas of work emerging all the time, for example child sexual abuse and AIDS, and these new developments can cause social workers a great deal of confusion and anxiety. The response of some workers and departments is to withdraw into a more traditional role.

But social work and social workers need to continue extending themselves for both personal and professional reasons. I will take the personal reasons first. Social work today is a seemingly impossible job. The bureaucracy appears intent on hampering a social worker's every move by, for example, insisting she keeps records and then not getting them typed. A social worker is continually trying to retrieve something from the mess created by, for example, the lack of humane policies on homelessness. Many social workers who have been working at basic-grade level for a few years also find they are emotionally exhausted on account of dealing, or sometimes failing to deal, with the same type of problem again and again. There is a need in us to refresh ourselves and to be creative in our work. One way of doing this is to develop a special interest which, of course, may not be anything to do with community work.

The professional reason why the work needs to develop is that if something stands still it stagnates. Many organisations are fighting today's problems with yesterday's ideas. A social services department which insisted on providing large communal homes for old people rather than co-operating with the housing authority to provide sheltered accommodation, at least as well as providing its traditional service, would be a backward department. But it is easy to do what one has always done and hard to innovate. The implications of a community social work approach are, therefore, that it should lead to agency change and that this too needs to be a concern of community social workers.

For social workers who wish to become involved in community work proper, the preceding chapters are most relevant. But how does a worker go about the work and what problems does she face, if she only wishes to use the community to extend and improve her social work practice? Once the relevant managerial arrangements have been made, which may take a great deal of time and effort, the next step might be for the team to conduct a relevant community /issue profile. The team may be most interested in data such as the numbers of children at risk and it will probably be necessary to research the existing community-support networks: playgroups, child-minders, etc. Ways then need to be found of keeping in contact with what is going on in the locality by meeting with local activists or other relevant people or organisations from time to time.

Of course this work is time consuming and it is possible to do only so much. But one afternoon per week is better than nothing, and team members should divide this community contact-making between them. There are, of course, a variety of ways of developing contacts. A worker could offer to do one session a week in an advice centre, for example. But it is important to be careful at this stage about taking on too much. That is why the team's involvement has to be carefully planned and strategic.

Patch social workers operating as community social workers soon find that they know quite a few people in the area who provide information which helps them in their work. They may then begin to see themselves as merely part of the support system for a particular client, rather than the sole agent who can help her solve her problems. Consequently, when a particular need arises the worker not only thinks of other ways to meet it besides the more conventional ways, but also has other contacts who can help in the problem-solving process. Thus, social workers may start referring some of their cases, or aspects of them, to their new contacts in the community. And these contacts start referring aspects of the cases with which they cannot deal to the social worker.

However, the next thing that happens is that more work is generated. The worker is able to offer through her new contacts a more comprehensive service, but begins to realise that she has just taken the lid off a bottomless pit of need. The difficulty is that there is no way of extending and developing the job without creating extra demands on oneself and one's agency. The rewards can be great as far as the satisfaction of having played a part in improving the service is concerned, but the price paid can be high. No wonder many individuals and agencies take as low a profile as they can. They fear, rightly, that if they did otherwise they would be creating demands they could not meet. This is understandable but it leads to a narrow approach where workers and agencies will leave undone as much as they can get away with, and will forget about meeting need. The other way does involve increased demands, and if we cannot meet them we have to say so. That is why a strategy is so vital. But increasing demands can make an agency look at what it is doing and consider different ways of doing it, as well as creating the pressure for extra resources, which can often be found if the will is there even during times of economic stringency. To make community social work effective good team work is vital. Yet social workers are not famed for their teamwork. (See Payne, 1982, for some ideas on how to work better in teams.)

There is another kind of stress. Once outside the bounds of the normal professional relationship we are less secure. We question established practices and try to respond to a range of needs over and above those which come as referrals. We may occasionally be called off the street to advise on a problem. We may be asked to transport furniture, to arrange a holiday, to set up a group for unemployed teenagers. What should a worker do when she meets requests like this? Even if we say we cannot help, do we feel it our duty to find someone who can? A worker can quickly find that she has an enormous informal caseload and that she is dabbling in a great many areas, all of which require more time if they are to be undertaken properly. How, if at all, should she record this work? How does she react when an informal contact complains that she is spending a lot of time with Mrs Jones (one of her 'regular' cases) and hardly any with her? The question of confidentiality can also be a factor. If Mrs Brown is to be involved as volunteer in helping her neighbour Mr Smith, how much confidential information should the worker give Mrs Brown?

We are more vulnerable when we branch out into community social work. We need to be fairly hard-headed and have worked out what we are doing, within a team framework. Being able to say 'no' becomes even more important, as does careful planning of what we are and are not prepared to take on. That is why we also need our agency's backing and a clear support structure.

Finally, as it takes a long time to get to know the area and build up trust among people, a worker needs to be prepared to stay in the job for a reasonable amount of time. I would say that three years is the minimum.

4

The Community Development Process III: Wider Considerations

Participation in voluntary action

Factors preventing people joining groups

Sociological analysis has emphasised divisions of class, and more recently, of gender and race. There are, however, many more subtle differences between groups of people which can also be significant, and a community worker needs to understand them. For instance Jamaicans might prefer not to mix with Barbadians. And on most council estates there is a 'rough–respectable' split (see Lupton and Mitchell, 1954). As regards who participates in what, such differences are at least as important as other class differences. If the first people who are recruited or who select themselves for a particular community activity are from one 'sub group', the 'roughs' for instance, the 'respectables' will not come and vice versa. Whatever activity is started it will quickly attract a label or image which, in effect, prevents other people from participating. In addition, people think of their 'home area' as very local, encompassing only a few streets and, perhaps for that reason, it is common for meetings of community groups to be attended only by people who live less than a quarter of a mile from the meeting place, and several of them will already know each other. All these factors inhibit wider attendance at meetings and tend to increase the cliquishness of a group.

All the members of a community may share the same problem at a general level but may want different solutions.

While all people in bad housing will want better housing, for some. that will mean a transfer but for others it will mean improvement of existing property. Even when the objective is clear, people differ as to how it should be achieved. The differences are often so great as to ensure that only those whose methods are adopted stay in the group.

The forces keeping people in community groups are weak compared with the forces keeping people in family groups, or at a place of work for example. Even the most committed members of community groups are usually more concerned about their personal and work lives than about their community activity, and we must all cope with illness, childbirth, divorce, bereavement and so on. It is easy for a community worker to forget that she does not own the soul of the community activist. During a crisis which occurred between two bingo-group leaders with whom I worked, one of them was also about to be evicted for non-payment of rent which, as would be expected, took precedence over her community concerns. Nevertheless, for some people the community group can assume an importance which may seem somewhat out of proportion. For example, the chair of the disabled club with whom I worked once told me he had spent two successive nights awake trying to work out the cheapest way of arranging an outing for the members.

Why do people participate?

The first law of participation is that people participate for what they can get out of it. If a community worker wants to avoid frustration she should not expect people, including her colleagues, to be very altruistic. She might work for two years with little success trying to organise a group to take up a range of environmental problems. Then a minor newspaper article suggests some waste land may be used as a gypsy site. Overnight an organisation forms in the same area and quickly organises a twenty-four-hour picket of the proposed site. Even in cases where the action taken is not so illiberal the basis for bringing people together is self-interest. Once people have had their own needs met they *may* then consider the needs of others, but often they drop out once their own problem has been solved. Even if people are altruistically motivated, personal interest and the likelihood of personal satisfaction will probably dictate their area of involvement. Our job is to understand their motivation and to help them find a means of expression. In that process the relationship we establish with them is of considerable importance.

How far do the poor participate?

Gallagher (1977) has argued that, in dire situations, deprived or oppressed people, and particularly women, are prepared to take leadership roles. They fight, probably because they have nothing to lose. If this is true, the implication is that the really poor, deprived or oppressed may join together in collective action if they are oppressed enough. But if the oppression is not too severe the worker may have to work very slowly, by arranging social activities for example, and gradually build up their motivation and confidence. (See also Piven and Cloward's book *Poor People's Movements* for a persuasive account of why disruptive action works.)

Vertical participation

Participation by ordinary people in activities run by the community is sometimes called horizontal participation. Participation in organisations or events which are primarily the responsibility of government can be seen as vertical participation. Examples of vertical participation would be Community Health Councils, tenant consultative committees, local enquiries into structure plans or parent representation on the managing bodies of schools. There are, however several different kinds of vertical participation. At its lowest level government merely informs a community, about the closing of a road for instance. At the other levels vertical participation involves consultation prior to a decision being taken, and joint action and devolved power where the community makes its own decision on a particular matter.

Vertical participation (see Taylor *et al.*, 1976, Richardson, 1983, Brager and Specht, 1969), is highly problematic, both because government often purports to consult when it really wants to manipulate and because community groups mostly want, and sometimes think they have got devolved power, when they are merely being consulted. While effective and meaningful vertical participation is vital in a democracy very clear thinking indeed is required before community groups become involved in such processes. This is because they are usually powerless partners who, if their members are not very watchful, can be used merely to legitimate decisions which would have been taken anyway and which may not be in the community's interest.

Understanding and influencing group processes

Community groups often find it difficult to take decisions. I have been to many meetings where hours have been spent discussing such mundane matters as whether new coffee cups should be bought. One reason for this is that in some groups the members unconsciously hope to take every decision by consensus. One way to help a group to deal with this is to encourage members to vote occasionally. When groups do take decisions this is often done in such a clumsy way that that misunderstandings occur as to the nature of the decision, which in turn alienates some members. A group with which I was associated discussed making a grant of £10 to another organisation but decided, I thought, to defer the matter until the next week. At the next meeting the matter was not mentioned until a member raised it, only to find that the treasurer had already paid over the money! The treasurer had thought the decision had been taken the previous week. The worker's job is to anticipate conflict like this and, if appropriate, to intervene to ensure that everyone knows the decision, particularly if minutes of meetings are not kept.

It can also be difficult to get a word in when the issue under discussion is particularly emotive. One way for a worker to deal with this is to have a word with the chair beforehand saying there is a particular point she wants to raise. Also, when a controversial item comes up unexpectedly, it is often a good idea to try to have the decision postponed and perhaps deferred to another meeting, when people will have had time to think about it. Otherwise a decision may be taken hurriedly which the group members regret. There will be other occasions when a group continually postpones a difficult decision and the worker may have to work both with individuals and the group as a whole to help the members to face this.

If a group does not accept an idea at one point this does not necessarily mean the members have forgotten about it. So we should be patient and continue 'sowing seeds', since we never know when they will bear fruit. It is important also to understand that people do not always act logically, at least as far as our logic is concerned. Let us say, for example, that the chair takes the minutes of the meetings. A suggestion that there should be a separate minutes secretary, which would be in her own interest, might well be rejected by her because it would upset her routine and could be perceived as a criticism.

Many needs are met in groups which are not to do with the stated aims of the group. If the stated aim of the group, to obtain a zebra crossing for example, requires a meeting once a month but the group is meeting weekly, the reason may be that the more frequent meetings meet expressive needs, which even the members do not recognise. When working with any group a worker can usefully ask herself which needs it is meeting and for whom, since meeting the unstated needs of some members, for approval perhaps, is likely to cause frustration for others.

Getting groups to evaluate

Learning by doing, which is what community work is about, inevitably involves some mistakes. Sometimes when groups make mistakes the lessons are obvious and the members change their behaviour, but not always. The need for a change in behaviour may be so threatening that the members are afraid to look at their mistakes. So they invent all sorts of rationalisations to explain them away. A community worker has responsibility to try to get the group to stand back and evaluate its achievements. Goetschius (1969, pp. 106-11), who has a useful section on helping a group to evaluate its work, comments that it is not enough merely to identify the mistakes. The members then have to decide how to alter their behaviour if they are to avoid repeating them.

When something which the worker predicted would go wrong does go wrong she needs to test out, in a calm atmosphere, whether the group members now understand how to avoid making the same mistake again. But, however, a worker does this, it is important not to expect the members to say she was right after all. Her satisfaction must be in seeing the changed behaviour, not in being given the credit. I always found it difficult to get a group to evaluate itself, and cannot make any clear recommendation in this respect. Ideally, I think, a worker should seek to establish a contract with a group which specifies that periodic reviews will be undertaken. However, this in turn depends upon workers negotiating more specific agreements with groups than is usually the case.

Without such an explicit agreement the worker may have to use other methods to get a group to change. For instance she may see that the group is being ineffective because Jack is doing all the work without prior approval by the committee. She can either raise this in the group or with individuals, or she can avoid the problem. If she has a good relationship with the group and if the commitment of Jack and the other members is high, they may be prepared to work at the problem and support Jack through it. But if commitment is not high she runs the risk of making herself unpopular to no avail. She might, therefore, have to restrict her role to making minor practical suggestions.

Making meetings work

Few people will attend meetings regularly which go on after 10 p.m., and, as the members have come to see business done, they will not be satisfied if the meeting does not complete this reasonably efficiently. So, meetings should be kept reasonably short. But the thoughts and feelings of members often do not coincide with items on the agenda; they would prefer to speak of a personal experience or tell a joke. Some allowance should also be made for people to express these feelings. If these expressive needs are not satisfied, the decision-making process may feel rather sterile and may ultimately not be satisfying enough to keep everyone in the group. If people are prevented from expressing their emotions in the group these emotions may become bottled up and expressed in some other way, for example in unreasoned opposition to a sensible proposal purely because it was made by a certain person. However, these emotional needs may conflict with the needs which are to do with taking decisions. Some group members are good at ensuring tasks are effectively undertaken, others are better at taking care of these 'socio-emotional' needs. But both are important. The worker has to try to find the right balance between getting the group to press on with the decision-making process and allowing people to express their feelings.

A further dilemma is to find tasks for the group which are fun, easy to do and unifying. Initially groups often begin to gel when the members work together. One occasion I enjoyed was when the carnival committee spent several evenings turning two rooms full of groceries into 1200 Christmas parcels for old people. There is a danger here though. Groups often concentrate on the tasks they enjoy rather than what they 'ought' to be doing. The carnival committee began with the purpose of running a carnival but found that it made money, most of which was disbursed to pensioners. Later the committee members spoke as if the rationale for the carnival was to raise money for pensioners. It had, perhaps, drifted into a changed set of objectives without being aware of the change.

Over-involvement

Many community leaders criticise others, their peers or the local authority perhaps, when they are failing adequately to carry out their own group responsibilities. This could be a signal that they need more help. A volunteer may be so involved in the youth club she is running that she opens it every night of the week, cannot cope, and has to reduce it to one day, thus creating frustratuon and aggression in the young people. The emotionally over-involved person is to a large degree meeting her own needs, and when problems arise she is likely to react as if she had been personally insulted, blaming the people for whose benefit she is supposed to be working. The enthusiasm turns to anger and a sense of martyrdom, and often the person gives up.

Another emotional reaction which the worker has to guard against is panic. From time to time, when groups organise events, for example public meetings, exhibitions or demonstrations, crises occur but they occur in particular combinations. The man providing transport for the older participants does not arrive, but Jane is going that way to collect the ice cream and agrees to do the job. Then she finds the ice cream shop was burgled the night before so she has to go to the other side of town and forgets to collect them. Many of us have a tendency during such crises to rush round madly, which not only adds to the panic but also increases the likelihood of decisions being taken which will create more crises. When we are under pressure we may not feel calm, but we have a calming effect on others if we can appear in control. This also applies to confidence. If a worker speaks confidently, even if she does not feel confident, she will find that she raises the confidence of those with whom she is in contact. Whatever the mood of the group, depressed or over-confident, it is iimportant for a community worker to maintain a degree of objectivity.

A worker also has to be aware of how other people perceive her and her project. Because we ran an advice centre we became tagged with a 'welfare' label, as a result of which some residents refused to come to our building. Because, as a community worker, I succeeded a very motherly, caring, female worker, some of the women with whom she had worked and to whom she had given a great deal of love were quite resentful that I was neither prepared nor able to do the same. To find out how we are seen we need to keep our eyes and ears open, but also to develop a range of contacts whom we can ask for feedback.

Building confidence

Our presence may also have a symbolic value for people. I am sure the fact that I was *their* worker and the neighbourhood centre was *their* project helped several people in the estate where I worked to feel that someone cared about them after all. Dora, for example, never came to our advice centre but I was told she always kept a list of our opening times in her purse. One effect created by the newsletter which we ran was a certain feeling of pride among some residents that their estate had one while others did not. We ignore at our peril these intangible aspects of our work, because they can make the difference between success and failure. Baldock writes (I paraphrase):

> By giving her approval the community worker can often legitimise in the eyes of local people an activity which they would not be sure was otherwise 'OK'. Thus, our recognition of their abilities is often important in developing their confidence. The fact that community workers are often 'educated' people from the 'Town Hall' gives us a status that many of us find embarrassing because it is not in unison with our aspirations and commitment to a more democratic and egalitarian society. However, we have to acknowledge that we often have that kind of status and cannot simply wish it away. (Baldock, 1989, from comments on first draft of the second edition of *Community Work*, 1989).

Mistakes

However thoroughly we plan our work we occasionally make mistakes. These are sometimes not only embarrassing but mean that a particular piece of work is endangered. For some months we had been trying to establish better relationships between our estate and the neighbouring estate. The adventure playground was due to be moved from the middle of our estate to a new site between the two estates. We had done some door-knocking on the neighbouring estate to tell people it was coming (informing, not consulting!), but this was not very thorough. When residents there opposed the move I tried to retrieve the situation by spending time with the key protester. I admitted that we were at fault since we had not discussed the matter with them earlier, and told her how she could oppose the move of the playground, at the same time saying that, as I was the chair of the playground, I could not support her.

When we have made a mistake we can often go some way to retrieving the situation, but we normally have to start by admitting our error. We are likely to have fewer problems in the long run if we are as honest as possible in this respect.

Dealing with conflict

Certain problems, particularly deep-seated conflicts between individuals, are not resolvable and it is of little use to try to resolve them. However, some workers have managed to help groups work through such difficulties. A worker with a group of tenants living in appalling accommodation found that personality differences between members were jeopardising the survival of the group. He confronted the group with the problem and pointed out that if the members continued to disagree violently they would never succeed in their campaign. After considerable discussion his point was accepted and the inter-personal conflict subsided somewhat. But he had a very high status in the group and the members were strongly motivated to keep the group together.

The inevitable prominence of some community leaders often generates a mixture of negative feelings among other group members. Indeed, any community activity will arouse some antagonism, which may be because most people are a little jealous of others and do not like to see them succeed. Some community leaders heighten jealousy or antagonism by making sure that it is always their photograph which appears in the paper, for instance. A worker must be careful not to fan smouldering jealousies.

I also wonder how far the idea which originated in counselling theory (Rogers, 1961) may be applicable in work either with community groups or, individually, with their leaders. Briefly put, Rogers argues that most clients in a counselling relationship (and in relationships generally) can work out their own solutions to their problems if they are fully accepted and not judged by the therapist and if the therapist tries to show she recognises their feelings by communicating the feeling which she thinks the client is experiencing back to them. This, among other approaches, provides the space for the client to solve her own problems. My own role as a community worker was always more 'pushy', interpretive and diagnostic than this. I might say, for example, 'Ted – if you want to get more members to participate in the group you are going to need to put issues to them in such a way that they can make real decisions'. I now think, however, that in some situations, particularly perhaps where progress is blocked through emotions rather than a lack of knowledge or skill, there may also be a place for a 'Rogerian' approach, or something like it.

When people are strongly committed to the groups with which they are involved, strong emotions can be aroused. People can feel vulnerable and exposed in groups, just as groups can also be enormously supportive. Two leaders of groups, both of which were running bingo sessions, once had an extremely vicious argument in another committee over a trivial matter. However, the real issue was that they each saw the other as a threat. Following that row, one of them telephoned the police to say that the other was running bingo illegally. Often such feelings do not come to the surface but if they exist, they are likely to have other detrimental effects.

At some stage most workers have to deal with personal hostility either from community members, residents, councillors or officials. Most people deal with it instinctively in one of two ways, either they hit back or they try to conciliate. It is generally advisable to 'soak up aggression' because retaliation means it is less likely we will gain the trust of the other person in the future. By this I mean not losing one's temper, considering whether there is anything in the criticism which is deserved, and apologising for that if it is appropriate to do so. However, at times it can be appropriate to show one's anger. If done rarely and with good reason, losing your temper can be very effective in getting what you want. I also believe that all community workers should understand and be able to apply the principles of assertiveness, which is neither aggression nor passivity nor manipulation, but an ability to say clearly that one's position is, what one wants and why. Once, when I was taken to task by two of my colleagues about failing to discuss a major proposal with them before agreeing it, part of me felt under personal attack. But in order to respond in a mature fashion I had to keep those feelings down and deal with the issue intelligently and unemotionally. I have found that as I become more secure personally I am more able to do this, rather than to react in a threatened way. For some of us this is not easy to learn, but it can be done.

Another useful way of dealing with situations involving personal criticism of yourself is to listen carefully to what is being said by the other party and to say you will let them have your response in a day or two when you have had time to think about it calmly.

Conflict is often the stimulus for change. A community organisation may be in the hands of an out-of-touch clique which enforces unpopular policies. Changing that situation involves conflict, and the worker's task might be to work with newer members to build up their confidence so that they will challenge the old guard. Or, if she was aware that feelings of dissatisfaction were present in the group, but found that no one was voicing the discontent, she might try to bring it out into the open in the group. Again, the degree to which a worker can do this successfully depends upon the nature of her 'contract' with the group.

It is also worth making the point that many of the people with whom community workers work have a conflict view in relation to the authorities., They perceive the council, sometimes correctly, as working against their interests. Part of the worker's job is to help them articulate this discontent. When people living in poor circumstances come together for the first time the anger expressed against the most likely target – usually the authorities, but sometimes it can be the worker or one of their own number – can be considerable. Be prepared for this and help them work through it. It is often a necessary step on the way to collective action. Beware, however, of people who are constantly critical of others. This may indicate that they are going to be very difficult to work with and may become very critical of the worker herself at a later stage.

There is no way a community group can make a significant contribution without coming into conflict at some point with the powers that be. But when groups first attempt to pressurise the authorities to change a policy or procedure the 'other side' often over-reacts. Councillors and officials become angry, and in turn try to pressurise the group to give up. That can be a difficult time, during which the group members require considerable support. But if groups can be helped to persevere, the authorities usually come to accept that the group is working in a particular way and will stop 'over-reacting'. In the long run they also often come to accept that the group is doing a useful job, and accept that a certain amount of conflict is not inappropriate.

There is also the question of keeping good relationships with people with whom one may be in conflict. The social services department had taken longer than a month to visit a client whom we had referred to the area office, and we decided to make a formal complaint. We were on friendly terms with the staff about whom we would be complaining and did not wish to jeopardise our relationship. Consequently, I telephoned the senior social worker, explained our concern and said that we were writing in about it. She did not like the fact that we were complaining but was grateful to have been informed and continued to co-operate with us on other matters.

Dealing with prejudice

The people we work with sometimes make what we may think are highly prejudiced statements about 'problem families', immigrants, itinerants and other minority groups, and expect our support. If you feel perplexed in these situations you are in good company! I once heard an experienced community relations worker explain what she did. She used to visit white groups and say something like, 'I hear you hate blacks. Let's hear about it.' After a stunned silence the floodgates would burst open and many extreme statements would be made. But there were always one or two people in the group who might say, 'but they've got to live somewhere', and at that point she was able to get the group discussing more rationally. This approach is consistent with Rogers' views about the nature of helping relationships in that the feelings of the group were recognised by the worker. I now try to make calm assertive statements about my own beliefs in such situations which other people can take or leave. I do not usually try to

persuade, though there are clearly times when oppressi
views have to be challenged.

Within any relationship manipulation can occur. At the
beginning of a meeting with housing officials in which there
was going to be some conflict a housing management assistant
paid a compliment to one of the residents. That resident told
me later that she felt this inhibited her from criticising the
housing department in the meeting. Ernie had let it be known
that he was thinking of resigning from a particular committee.
Fred, knowing I was in contact with Ernie, told me that he
and the treasurer, would resign if Ernie did, his unstated
objective being to get me to prevent Ernie from resigning. A
worker finds herself under considerable pressure of this
nature much of the time. Because emotional factors are
brought to bear the pressure can sometimes be difficult to
resist, but the best response is either a carefully thought out
one or no response at all.

A counselling role?

The question of how far a community worker should go in
offering counselling help to community members is difficult,
particularly if she is a new worker who is trying to establish
trust and rapport for the first time. When a worker finds that
the only problems some people are prepared to talk about are
personal she can easily find that she is assuming the role of
social worker, which should not happen. The main role of a
community worker with individuals is to help them learn how
to undertake aspects of collective action. That is essentially
different from a counselling role, where one is helping
somebody resolve personal difficulties. Nevertheless, there
are times when the worker is called upon to be a counsellor,
especially with residents with whom she is already closely
involved, and who may turn to her for personal help at a time
of crisis.

The effects of work with community groups

Being involved in community action can help some people
grow enormously and lead enriched lives, benefiting not only

their family life but also their career. It has been noted, for example, that community activists sometimes go on to become councillors and professionals. But there are numerous other examples, for instance the woman who for the last four years of her life was the secretary of a self help group for disabled people and who, on her own account, was happier than she had been during the previous ten years, in spite of increasing pain.

However, this positive effect seems only to occur to small numbers of people. In addition, working people often lose money by being involved in community groups; they take unpaid leave, subsidise the group or are unable to work overtime. Often the only way to run a community group successfully is to work intensively at it and there is no question that this sometimes causes breakdowns and marital stress. Another consideration is that being involved in community action often causes a person, a woman for example, to look at the world in a new way, and to begin to question her role as wife and mother. This is obviously an important growing process, but it can sometimes be traumatic too.

When people initiate a project, it is likely that they appropriated the idea from someone else in the first place. Community work and community action help to spread the idea that people can become involved in doing things themselves, and also show them by example what can be done. But this process is largely invisible, indirect and long term. People who are involved in community action probably also provide models for their children who later become involved in similar activities, just as elected representatives often have parents who were on the council. Nevertheless we cannot easily measure many of these changes. A linked point is that no one piece of community action should be viewed in isolation. In the area in which I was employed, several years work had been undertaken by my predecessor to help establish the carnival committee, within which were four or five very able community leaders. By the time of my arrival, some of these leaders were aware that many other community needs required attention. I encouraged them to think about these problems and two of them subsequently became leaders of other community groups. In encouraging these leaders, who subsequently left the carnival committee, I had contributed to the decline of the carnival, which I had not anticipated. The lesson is: think about the wider effects of a piece of action rather than merely the immediate effects.

There is also the question of arousing unrealistic expectations. If nothing can be done about a particular problem, is it worth encouraging people to get worked up about it? A certain local authority had planned a major road scheme to run through an inner-city area, demolishing several houses. Three weeks before the public enquiry, and after several houses had already been compulsorily purchased, residents formed an action group to oppose the scheme. But by then there was no chance of stopping the scheme. I raise this point, not because I believe we should never become involved in such a campaign, but because workers often dissipate their energies fighting battles they cannot win, while neglecting other tasks which might prove more fruitful.

It is clear that community groups can and do achieve significant objectives: play-schemes, care schemes, improvements to the environment, for example. But these changes are often more limited than the members hope they will be, and many groups die before achieving their stated objectives. A dispassionate analyst would probably conclude not only that the efforts put in far exceed the concrete achievements, but also that not many members of community groups develop personally either. But are there other achievements and why is it that community workers feel so strongly that collective action is good? One answer is as follows. There are often some positive outcomes which are not intended and which are not connected in the minds of most people with the existence of a particular group. Jim became chairman of the parent-teacher association (PTA). At the same time, two students doing practical work with me started a youth club, and when they were due to depart they found that he was willing to take over. He later started running a junior football team too. The PTA had provided a way in for him, first to fulfil himself more, and second to contribute to the community.

Community development encourages people to take positive action and to believe that they can act, that they can cause change, which can sometimes help to give their lives greater meaning. Of the lessons learned by the participants in community action perhaps the most important are new attitudes, new political perspectives and a broader understanding of how the world works. Grace, a single parent and community leader, told me that since our project had been running, she had learned to stand her ground with the housing management assistant and no longer let her walk into the house at will, for example. The carnival committee ran a reasonable carnival for a few years, as a result of which the area appeared on the front page of the local paper for positive reasons rather than because it was a 'debtors' haven'. This must have done a great deal to boost the self-esteem of residents. After running a complex community project involving many different organisations and which included, at one stage, an abseil down the church tower, one community leader said she was now ready to run General Motors which she thought would probably be easier!

Pressure from community groups alone does not seem to induce a governmental organisation to change a policy completely, though such pressure can help to modify governmental policies, especially if community groups forge alliances with other organisations which have wider influence. But community groups both of a pressure group and a service nature also have a longer term effect. The pre-school playgroup movement has, through the running of playgroups for the last twenty-five years, been influential in affecting thinking in Britain about the need for play. Also, campaigns against damp in council housing or for more women's refuges, though often unsuccessful in individual cases, have resulted in a recognition that certain types of house construction are faulty, and that there is an enormous amount of domestic violence. Thus, a 'battle' may be lost but the course of the war may nevertheless be influenced. I think that the major outcomes of community action, are the long term effects on the climate of opinion and on the self image of the main actors rather than their immediate concrete results. There is also to my knowledge, virtually no research in Britain which evaluates the longer term outcomes of community work and community action. For these reasons, and particularly because of the lack of concrete evidence about the results of our work, it is the faith of the community worker that our work is of value which must often sustain us, because concrete achievements may not.

5

Social Planning Approaches to Community Work

Introduction

While the uniqueness of community work lies, I believe, in the community development approach, the social planning approach is now more common. To complicate matters further, social planning is a wide field in itself, encompassing many other activities, such as economic planning and national planning, which have little to do with community work. Thus, on the one hand, most community workers are involved in social planning; on the other hand, most people who engage in social planning could not be described as community workers.

My use of the term 'social planning' within community work needs careful defining. I have always noticed community workers undertake many activities other than assisting community groups to run their own projects. This can range from doing minor things for groups all the way to planning and implementing large scale projects such as a community care scheme for mentally ill people across a borough. I use 'social planning' to describe all this work.

At a philosophical level, the idea that community workers work with 'the community' in a neutral way on issues determined by the community, is open to debate. We are all bound to seek out persons in the community with whom we think we can work and who want to undertake the activities which we think are the most valuable. Neither on the whole do communities choose us to work for them; we choose the community. From this standpoint, therefore, all community work includes elements of social planning, since the worker or agency inevitably plays a large part in deciding where the worker should work and what activities she should become involved with. Thus, to a greater or lesser extent, community work is not determined by the community but by the agency or its staff.

At a more practical level, there are three sets of activities which constitute a social planning approach within community work; doing work for groups (as opposed to acting as a facilitator), acting as an advocate or mediator with other organisations on an existing group's behalf, and undertaking an activity without reference to a community group. However, only the last of these could properly be called social planning: the first two are, perhaps, stages towards it, since the worker is no longer acting purely as an enabler.

Doing work for groups

Most community development workers undertake activities *for* the groups and organisations with which they work. This can include activities such as booking a room, undertaking a research project and even on occasion acting as chair, secretary or treasurer of the group, thus taking a leadership rather than an enabling role. It is my view that, properly carried out, undertaking activities *for* groups in this way, rather like being an ordinary member or leader, can strengthen the confidence, capacities and autonomy of group members, though, if it is done without due thought it can have the effect of making people dependent. Thus it should only be done for a limited time and preferably on the understanding that group members should take over that work at a later date, since the aim of a community development worker should always be to ensure that the members of the group learn how to undertake action themselves.

Acting as an advocate for a group

A worker often acts as an advocate when a group is unable to present its own case to another organisation. I once helped the secretary of an organisation for disabled people get the installation of a telephone paid for by the social services department after the organisation had applied and been refused. The case had not been presented well and inappropriate legislation had been cited. The application was only granted when I wrote to the department citing the appropriate legislation. In theory I could have helped the secretary write another letter appealing against the decision, but that might have taken some time, besides which the secretary had rather given up the struggle and might not have wished to write another letter. It was also important to get the decision reversed quickly.

A colleague of mine working in a local authority helped an organisation obtain its annual grant after it had been refused by the City Council. Again, the initial application had been badly presented by the group. Normally, the worker would have been present at the relevant local authority committee to speak for the organisation. However, he was ill and certain officials opposed to the organisation presented the application in an unfavourable light. Luckily he was able to bring the matter up at the next committee and got the decision reversed. It might be asked why could the worker not work with the secretary of this organisation to ensure that a well presented application was made in the first place. There are several reasons for this. First, he might not have been invited to help. Second, the secretary might have resented his interference if he had offered to help. Third, he could have been wrong; the application might have elicited the grant. Fourth, he was probably busy servicing several different groups and might not have had the time to do the necessary work with the secretary of the group to ensure a successful application. Finally, ensuring the organisation got its grant probably also required the use of contacts which only he had, by virtue of his position in the local authority. (This kind of work can also be called 'Fixing' or 'Working the System'.)

At a more general level Leo Smith's work is a good example of advocacy in practice. As 'Participation Officer' for a London borough his job was to ensure that community groups had good access to the local authority, and he spent a good deal of time working within the authority to ensure that appropriate access policies were initiated (L. Smith, 1981).

Another aspect to the advocacy role is that of the broker. Many workers reject the idea of acting in this way between the authorities and a community group because the worker's real purpose is to help a group negotiate on its own behalf and 'stand up' to the other organisation. But two different parties may often take issue over a matter because they see it from different points of view and cannot appreciate the perspective of the other. They then find themselves in fixed positions and do not listen to what the other has to say. For example, I once proposed to a voluntary organisation that the fieldwork teacher on our community work course at the university should be based part-time in the agency. The committee was hostile to the idea. They thought I was using them for my own ends, whereas I considered that I was doing them a good turn by offering them more staff resources!

This mismatch in thinking is continually happening between community groups and the outside world and often results in unnecessary frustration and failure. The worker's role is to help explain the perception of one party to the other, to identify clearly the point at issue and if possible to bring the parties together to resolve it. However, a lot of preparatory work sometimes needs to be done before the parties are brought together and it can only work if they both want it. Goetschius (1969, pp. 93–5) has a useful section on the steps to take when acting in this way.

Acting as advocate or broker has many dangers. The danger of making groups dependent on the worker is ever present; it is so often quicker for the worker to do the job herself, and the resulting outcome so obviously to the immediate benefit of the group, that 'product' can become more important than process. Yet the uniqueness of community development is that ordinary people learn to do things for themselves. A related danger is that the worker slides into the role of mediator or even buffer between the community group and the target organisation. On reflection I think I acted in this way during the incident mentioned in Chapter Three when I explained to the members of a group with which I was working that it was no use seeking permission to use a football pitch on a Sunday because local authority policy forbade this. When its members did not accept what I said I found myself trying to persuade them. Thus, I was, in effect representing the position of the local authority to the group. I now think that it would have been more appropriate to put the group members in touch with the local authority in order for them to discover the reality for themselves and, perhaps, to change the policy. If the worker does not do this she runs the risk of acting as an apologist for the target organisation. Also, she is protecting public officials from coming into direct contact with the consumers of services and from explaining and justifying their policies. Community workers can also sometimes become quite pessimistic about the possibilities of change and may overestimate the difficulties. Often a great deal can be achieved when the group members are enthusiastic and apply political pressure themselves.

Advocacy on behalf of a community group should normally only be undertaken with the knowledge and consent of the group. The aim should also be to try to ensure that the group acts as its own advocate. However, community workers who are in contact with a range of officials and politicians have many opportunities to influence the political and administrative process to the advantage of the communities with which they work – by ensuring that details of new funding arrangements are widely circulated, or to speak up in favour of particular groups at a particular meeting for example – and it would be foolish not to take those opportunities when they arise.

Thus, the community development worker who also acts as an advocate is, in a certain sense, working at two levels; within the community, but also with the target organisation, the policies of which the community group wishes to affect. She is working 'at both ends' of the change process.

The essence of advocacy is, I believe, the ability of the worker to put herself in the place of both parties. Presumably the worker understands the position of the community group. But she also needs to understand the reasons, from the 'opposition's' point of view, why the particular request is not able to be granted. Only then is it possible to describe the request in terms which the 'opposition' might find acceptable.

At a higher level some organisations which operate in social planning ways are primarily advocacy or social action organisations rather than service organisations. Examples would include the National Tenants' Organisation and its regional affiliates, the (national) Child Poverty Action Group, Shelter (the national campaign for homeless people) and CLEAR (the campaign for lead free petrol). However, such organisations may decide to undertake their advocacy in one of two ways or in both. On the one hand they may act as community development agencies in that they promote citizen participation and mobilise ordinary people around the issue in question. On the other hand their staff may undertake research, publish reports, lobby politicians and so on, primarily without involving their constituency, thus taking a social planning approach to advocacy.

Direct work with service providers and policy-makers

The community work role of initiator or social planner was once described quite well to me by a director of social services. He said, 'It's useful to have people like you employed without a particular service responsibility because you have the time to look at needs on the ground and find new ways of meeting them'. That is how community workers spend much of their time. They set up law centres, youth employment schemes, women's refuges, to name but a few. However, this role requires a range of specific skills. First, we have to analyse needs and identify how these can be met. Second, we need the interactional and organisational skills necessary to bring people together, and to motivate them to work on problems, and find and implement solutions. Third, we need the skills of project planning and management. The reason for this is that when we are involving other professionals, as we usually do, it is likely that the project will be complex requiring careful planning and managing and the recruitment and supervision of paid or unpaid staff.

The social planning role in community work applies most directly when the work undertaken by the worker has no direct and immediate link with a community group. For instance, if a community group goes out of existence the worker may decide to continue working on the issues which the group was taking up, but under the auspices of her own agency or with a group of professionals. I once acted in this role when a tenants' association, which I had helped establish, collapsed. It had been concerned with the modernisation of council houses, and I thought it important that the work it was doing should be continued. I took this issue further by carrying out a survey of tenant satisfaction with the houses which had already been modernised and fed back the results to the housing department in order to seek to affect policy. In that particular case I found that tenants had not been satisfied with the amount of tenant consultation over the modernisation and recommended that the housing department participate in a 'housing liaison group' with tenants in order to discuss housing policy. Thus, I used a social planning approach to return to a community development approach.

On other occasions an opportunity to provide a necessary service may arise when a community group does not exist and it may not be appropriate to try to bring one into existence. I once attended a social worker's lunch club and heard the head of the (City) Family Planning Association (FPA) suggest the need for a local clinic. There were a number of very large families in the neighbourhood and I thought that a locally run clinic might well serve the needs of the local people better than the city centre one. So, liaising with the FPA, local GPs and health visitors I arranged for family planning advice to be provided one day per week at the existing well baby clinic. This process was quite easy, and a reasonably well run family planning service was provided within a short period of time.

If I had wanted to take a community development approach to this problem I could have spoken with local people to see if they agreed that there was a need and were interested in trying to get such a clinic. This process would almost certainly have been a longer one and may not have worked since, when a worker starts with an issue or activity which interests *her*, it does not always prove possible to ensure that an autonomous community group forms to take it up.

I once discussed consumer participation with a friend who is also a district councillor, the context being tenant management of council housing. I suggested that recent legislation made it possible for council tenants to turn their estates into housing co-operatives. His reply was 'We'll give the estates over to tenants to form co-operatives any time they want. But what they want is a good service and not be bothered with running their estates themselves.'

In general terms I think he's right. I want to enjoy myself in my spare time, and so do most of us. But I also think that if consumers are not involved in some major way in influencing the services they receive those services deteriorate. Therefore, as people are often not able or prepared to participate in influencing those services it makes sense for community workers in some situations to work with other professionals to improve them.

Community workers, by virtue of their ability to build organisations themselves, their ability to help others build organisations, their ability to communicate and their personal knowledge of and contact with the people of the community they serve, are in a perfect position to influence service development. Demographic changes (for example an ageing population), legislative changes, the frequent though often short-lived availability of funds for specific purposes, new fashions in social policy (for instance, community care or job training for young people) all require social entrepreneurs who can work with others to develop appropriate organisations. These entrepreneurs (read community workers) need not only organisational skills but also a value system which is rooted in a desire to meet the real needs of people in the community and to involve them in planning and running their services whenever possible, thus 'empowering' them.

In the past community workers sometimes spoke arrogantly about other professionals and tended to refrain from working with them, the accusation being (and I exaggerate somewhat) that service professionals were lackeys of an oppressive system and that by collaborating with them one was colluding with the oppression of the people one was trying to help.

This sometimes went together with an implied scorn for those members of our society who could not be economically active, as community workers sought to work with the relatively easy to organise, public sector tenants in particular. Baldock (1982) makes this point eloquently and suggests there is a major role for community workers in working with high need groups such as older or handicapped people.

Thankfully, today, however, experienced community workers realise that helping community groups obtain real power is extraordinarily problematic, difficult and slow, that such groups can oppress other groups, that community work has indeed been 'incorporated' by the state (Waddington, 1979), that there are no easy answers regarding the kind of society to be striven for, that it is as important to change ideas as it is to bring about structural change, that the disadvantaged people with and for whom we work want better services *now*, and finally, that our own meal tickets are nearly all provided by a state which, at least ostensibly, wants us to develop services to high need groups. It is, thus, a legitimate and appropriate role for community workers to use pretty much the same organisation building skills which we use in the community development process to work with other professionals to build organisations providing services for high need groups. Indeed I consider one hallmark of an effective community project to be the degree which it has assisted a variety of professionals to collaborate.

One way to start this collaborative process is for a community worker to liaise with other professionals on a regular basis and to structure this into her work plan. When good contacts are made, in the long run, better ways are found of using resources and of collaborating over new ventures.

Establishing good contacts with other professionals requires, first, an ability to empathise, and, second, a concern to assist them with their work if at all possible. If one is genuinely interested in how 'the other' sees the world and is concerned to improve services it is not usually difficult to establish good relationships. However, one also finds that different professionals all see a situation slightly differently. This is because their assumptions, their starting points are all different. That is why, in my view, professionals from different agencies have so much difficulty working together. Most of us (and this includes community workers too) are able to see the world only from their own perspective. If we aim to work with other professionals to bring about changes, then we need first of all to see the world their way; starting where they are! (See Bayley, 1985, for an elaboration of the difficulties of inter-agency work and some guidelines as to how to go about it). It is also important for each worker in, say, an inter-agency liaison group to explain the 'mission' of her own organisation initially and to explain how she sees the issues in question. Then, at least, each agency has an opportunity to understand how the others perceive the situation. If this is not done the group is likely to get bogged down with people talking at cross purposes due to conflicting but unstated assumptions.

Evidence to support the proposition that community workers can act effectively in social planning ways can be found in Corina (1977). He looked at the influences on local authorities and concluded that the influence of community groups was minor. But he also concluded that contact with middle rank local authority officers was one of the most effective ways of obtaining influence. Other, more indirect evidence is provided by Levin (1981) who describes the process by which a local authority took a decision to build a major housing scheme. There was no point at which a firm decision to go ahead with the project was made; the local authority gradually found itself committted to it. Only by being involved on a continuing basis before any decisions were taken would it have been possible to alter the course of events. Community workers, especially those working in governmental organisations, are often in an excellent position to take the necessary action to influence such processes.

There are also several occasions when all the consumers of a service cannot be consulted in advance such as in the above example. In such cases, and there are many of them, it is, I think, the responsibility of the professional worker to act as advocate for the 'community' which does not yet exist in a real way.

A social planning approach in practice
Some examples of social planning
Here are just a few examples of a social planning approach to community work:

(a) devising a constitution for a new community organisation;
(b) working with councillors and the leaders of local organisations to establish a community association for a small town;
(c) bringing professional workers together to set up an adventure playground;
(d) setting up a rape crisis line;
(e) running a conference;
(f) producing an information sheet for parents of children with a mental handicap;
(g) setting up a branch of CHAR (The Campaign for the Homeless and Rootless);
(h) setting up an AIDS helpline.

Service strategies and influence strategies in social planning

Some such projects, CHAR for example, would be pressure group or campaigning projects where the driving force was professional workers, some of whom would be working in a personal capacity while others worked in their professional capacity. Such a group might also involve consumers. However, my own experience of work with severely disadvantaged people is that they often, though not always, lack the skill and motivation to become involved in running a sophisticated campaign and need a great deal of individual assistance to be able to participate alongside professionals.

Many community organisations are involved both in service strategies and influence strategies. For instance, Age Concern groups in Britain are involved in establishing projects such as hospital discharge schemes, but they also attempt to influence governmental policy with regard to the needs of older people.

Usually campaigning organisations which are set up under a social planning approach are not successful in obtaining funds to employ personnel to run the campaign because few funding organisations will provide resources for campaigns. Thus, the majority of projects set up by means of a social planning approach are service projects, and some of them obtain resources to employ staff. To take the previous example, the CHAR group which was orginally a campaigning group, might successfully apply for resources to establish accommodation for homeless people and thus become a new service agency. In such cases the community worker who was a member of the CHAR group or was servicing it would be involved in designing and possibly managing the new service.

In the future in Britain, when voluntary organisations may provide 'community care' or other services on a contractual basis they may have to decide whether to become either service organisations or consumer organisations. It may not be possible for them to be both.

Community workers adopting social planning approaches may, in effect, create or work with organisations of professionals. In today's world many important issues bridge several disciplines. Play, for example, relates to recreation departments, education departments, and social services departments. If a worker is trying to effect a change she is bound to be operating in these areas of interjacence. Therefore she will need to spend time as a member of inter-departmental or inter-professional bodies. Sometimes these bodies will be *ad hoc* and temporary, such as working parties, or they will be more formal organisations consisting of professionals, councillors, and representatives of voluntary bodies. Sometimes no formal body will exist but the worker will be involved with a range of organisations in order to facilitate a policy change or to implement a new procedure. However, it is the neighbourhood organisation consisting of professionals which I now wish to consider.

The 'professional' neighbourhood organisation

A powerful force for change on the estate when I worked as a fieldworker was an umbrella organisation consisting of professionals. It had initially been established as an organisation for professionals by the vicar and the children's officer, with the purpose of examining needs in the locality, but it later included representatives of community groups. I became a member of that organisation but also acted as its chief executive in that I carried out what it decided should be done, for instance organising a newsletter. A community worker in Cardiff set up an action group of professionals with sub-committees on environment, play, health, old people, and so on. The sub-groups each worked on their own specific areas and implemented different schemes. There are also many other examples.

When forming an organisation for professionals at neighbourhood level there are the usual problems of inertia, apathy even, yet it is usually easy to set up informal meetings, say over lunch. The problem with these kinds of meetings is that the liaison is 'passive' rather than 'active'. In order for a group of professionals to stay in existence an activity is needed which they can all work on. But they will each have their special interests and if the group decides to undertake a project to benefit older people, schoolteachers, for example, are unlikely to be interested. The answer is to find a project or series of projects which fire the interest of a reasonable number of the professionals in the area. Corina (1977, pp. 74–8) gives an interesting example of area councillor committees which consisted of councillors, officers and residents, and which were able to discuss policy matters before the council took firm decisions. Newcastle's Priority Area Teams are another example. Such organisations are worth considering because they have great potential not only for getting things done at local level but also for acting as vehicles of agency change, in that the professional automatically has a foot in her own agency as well as in the field.

However, such groups of professionals often fail to allow residents to articulate their needs, and I would be very concerned about such a group which did not try to create effective resident participation and to allocate adequate resources for this.

Specialist community work and social planning

The frame of reference within which this chapter has so far been written is mainly that of the generic neighbourhood community worker. I have argued that such workers need to engage both in community development and in social planning. But what of the specialist community worker who is concerned with a community of interest: what should her role be?

While in neighbourhood level community development there is some danger that the worker will not use a social planning approach enough, the danger for most specialist community workers, especially those working in statutory agencies, is that they will not engage in community development at all. This is because, increasingly, statutory agencies are employing staff, who are mostly not called community workers but who require the same skills, in order to develop services for high need groups. Examples of this work could include: establishing small group homes for disabled people who were being discharged from long stay institutions, setting up a drugs advisory service, establishing an alternative to custody for young people in trouble, running a 'priority estates project' on a stigmatised housing estate.

In such work the starting point is not what the community wants, but what the service agency wants. There is, however, a paradox here. On the one hand a new service of this kind will not work well unless the consumers are involved in deciding what it should be. On the other hand they will not easily become involved if it is a 'top down' service with a minimal amount of consumer consultation, which is what specialist community work is usually expected to be by the service providers. This creates difficulties for the worker because it often proves impossible to involve the consumers on this basis.

Specialist community workers employed by non-statutory agencies, such as Women's Aid, Shelter, legal advice centres, the Pre-school Playgroups' Association, housing associations, common ownership development agencies, community relations councils, Mind, Mencap, Age Concern and the like, often have more freedom, in principle, to use community development as well as social planning approaches. However, most of these agencies are funded by government to provide services and they only receive their annual grant on this basis. Also, their staff often operate over too wide an area for any in-depth community development to be undertaken. So, in practice, their freedom may also be limited.

With specialist community work relating to a community of

interest the distinction between community development and social planning often breaks down, and the role of the worker can also become confused. As a neighbourhood worker one can walk the streets, get into contact with ordinary people and start the community development process. Differences of social class, housing tenure, educational attainment, occupation, culture and the place they live will usually separate the worker fairly distinctly from the neighbourhood community in which she works. Thus, it is easy for the worker to know when she is working with other professionals or councillors rather than the local people. The corresponding community development approach with a community of interest is to get into contact with people in need either through their representatives (for example the parents of children with a mental handicap) or through the people who work with them, doctors, teachers, social workers, etc. However, when promoting self help groups of which the prime purpose is to provide mutual support for people sharing a particular need or circumstance, it is often the case that 'professionals' are also ordinary members of the group because they share the same condition. For instance a community worker once set up a support group for cancer sufferers. While one of the leaders was a health visitor who was there in a professional capacity she also had cancer.

When a specialist community worker moves from getting up an expressive (self help) group (as in the above example) to setting up an instrumental group it often becomes even more difficult to distinguish between consumers and professionals. The case of mental handicap provides a classic example. A county-wide organisation was established by a community worker working for a social services department, the purpose of which was to take various actions to improve housing opportunities for people with a mental handicap. The majority of the committee consisted of parents (let us consider parents as consumers at this point, though they are primarily the representatives of the consumers). Several of those parents had been active volunteers with Mencap for years and were very experienced – in many cases more 'professional' than the social services staff. One of them was now also employed by Mencap. Another worked part-time in an Adult Training Centre. Other members of the committee included a bank manager (who acted as treasurer) and representatives from the health authority. On this particular group there were no people with a mental handicap. The two social services department representatives (community workers specialising in mental handicap) were also full members of the group. But one of them had a child with a mental handicap. Thus, this organisation contained a mixture of consumers and professionals some of whom were there in several capacities.

In specialist work with communities of interest the important distinction between community workers (or the community work agency) and the community group or organisation which they are servicing often also becomes blurred. For instance, the development of a voluntary Age Concern group in a small town may have been fostered by a paid community worker. The group might then go on to acquire its own resources in order to employ a development worker. This worker would probably act not only as the general secretary of the organisation, running the services it provided, but also as a community development worker helping other groups concerned with the needs of older people to emerge at a more local level. Thus, an increasing number of organisations now exist which have paid staff and which are both service agencies and community development agencies at the same time.

The roles professional community workers are called upon to play in such groups can be conflicting and confusing. On the one hand, by using her 'enabling' skills the community worker may have brought other members together to form the organisation. On the other hand she may also play a major organisational role and be in effect the secretary or chair of the group. Yet, playing the two roles well at the same time is virtually impossible.

In such a group the worker might, in addition, share the same circumstances or condition as the 'ordinary' group members (for example have a mentally handicapped child). On this point it is noticeable that the motivation of professional community workers or other welfare workers is, in many cases, related to personal experience, of oppression, bereavement, or some other difficult personal circumstance.

As we saw earlier, the roles of enabler and organiser or leader are difficult to combine. In the organisation mentioned above, which was concerned with housing for people with a mental handicap, the social services department also provided funding and other resources, which were not always adequate. The unfortunate community workers had to cope with being members of the group and, probably, sharing the criticisms which the group members had of their employing organisation, and yet, also being the spokespersons for the social services department which they could not easily criticise openly. Clear thinking, careful planning and excellent communication skills are necessary to handle the problems which arise with such organisations.

It is also a mistake to think that professionals know how to operate in groups and organisations. Generally speaking, groups of professionals suffer from most of the same problems as groups of ordinary members of a community, though not always to the same degree.

From social planning to community development?

In thinking about different approaches to community work it helps, in my view, to move conceptually from the ideas central to community development, towards the notion of social planning. As we saw, however, most employers of community workers today, especially those in the statutory sector, are more concerned with service development than with involving the consumer. Thus, the way into community development for many professional workers may be through social planning. The Take Care project run by the Wales Council for Voluntary Action aimed to repair the homes of poor elderly owner occupiers. Resources from the EEC and Manpower Services Commission were used to employ people without jobs to do the work, but a planning group of service providers was also set up which also lobbied government and other agencies. From direct contact with the client group a number of community groups were also set up consisting, in the main, of older people in order to oversee the scheme in each locality. This mechanism allowed local people both as service providers and as consumers to meet to discuss their problems with the main service providers. This is an example of one of the many ways in which community workers operating as social planners can also bring a community development focus to their work.

Confusing community development and social planning

When, as a neighbourhood community worker, I was involved with the anti-motorway campaign mentioned earlier I initally thought I was doing community development. I thought I was helping local residents run their campaign. It was only when I discovered that I was doing all the work I realised that those involved saw me as the leader or organiser. They would follow but they would not lead. I found myself caught between two conflicting roles – organising, because it was important to try to stop the motorway, and enabling, because I wanted them to do it. When I realised this I judged that, in this case, product was more important than process, and, since time was short, led, which is what they wanted me to do. But the residents involved did not learn as much about organising against a motorway as they probably would have if they had run the campaign themselves.

Dilemmas of social planning

The danger of a community development worker moving into social planning is that she is to some degree forsaking one of the first principles of community work, namely, 'starting where people are at'. She runs the risk of merely getting done what she wants to see done, ignoring what members of the community want, and failing to involve them in the process. She may also find that the business of co-ordinating and managing the projects she sets up takes all her time and prevents her from giving much attention to 'community-centred' activities which may not be so productive in terms of concrete achievements. Therefore, when we initiate schemes without reference in the first instance to a community group, we must ensure that we still spend time on 'community-centred' activity and seek to involve members of the community whenever appropriate.

If we have assessed needs correctly, and if we set up the project properly, there is likely to be considerable community support for schemes which we initiate. However, there are so many needs which require meeting and so few members of the community who are prepared and able to meet them, that it is unrealistic to expect those people to take up everything, which is borne out by the following story.

A community worker in the USA was helping residents of what in Britain we would call a caravan site to buy their homes collectively and set up a management co-op. The committee members seemed reluctant to see the process through until the worker told them they could employ somebody to collect rents, undertake repairs etc. They had, quite understandably, balked at the implications that they would have to undertake all the necessary work on an unpaid basis.

It also needs to be remembered that there is a 'community work' way and a 'non-community work' way of going about meeting needs. Here is an example of the non-community work way. A worker identified a need for youth provision in the locality and set up a youth club one evening per week. It went well, so he opened two, three, four, five nights per week. Then he found he had become a youth worker! A true community worker would approach the problem in a different way. Perhaps she would start a club one evening per week to reveal the need and show what could be done. But she would spend the rest of her time trying to involve others, church organisations, residents or the district youth officer for example, in creating a mechanism whereby others would take responsibility at a certain point so that she could withdraw and move on to something else.

To get others to take responsibility for a project is often more difficult than it seems, however. For instance, we may argue the case with potential funders for resources, but with no success. Ultimately we may decide to run the project, perhaps in our spare time, to show that it works. Then when the project is running, our own agency or possibly another agency, may take an interest and adopt it as a matter of policy. But unfortunately, to obtain these kinds of changes is often very difficult. Many agencies will allow us to develop our own special interest, but will let it die when we leave. If we want it to continue, we must also work to structure the change we have initiated into the agency or other agencies. A basic principle to follow at all levels of work is that, if we want to implement a change which will involve another party, we must make sure we involve that party at an early stage of the planning. Thus, they will have done the thinking with us and will not feel they are being presented with an 'all or nothing' decision later on, which is just the way to stiffen their resistance.

The case against social planning

Community work is essentially about assisting communities to gain the capacity to see that their needs are met. The legitimation of the community development worker comes from the fact that she is in regular face to face contact with ordinary members of the community on whose behalf she is working and that she is helping at least some of them do what they want to do. The community development process is premised on the idea that people mainly learn how to do things by trial and error. If I always tie my son's shoelaces for him he will never learn how to do so himself. Thus, getting involved in direct service provision, even if the services benefit the community means, at best, that the worker is not spending time on the informal adult education process we call community development. At worst, the community worker can actually be destructive, since some of the services which community workers are hired to promote are misconceived, under-resourced, exploit the consumer and generally dis-empower communities. Another danger is that, getting involved in schemes which involve volunteers at the same time as services are being cut back can mean that, in a sense, community workers are colluding in a process whereby certain necessary jobs, in domiciliary services for example, are reduced. One can legitimately ask who benefits in such situations.

Welfare pluralism, community corporations and the private sector

A related but much wider topic is that of welfare pluralism, namely the idea that a plurality of sources, not just government, should deliver welfare. They would include the private sector, the family, the informal sector (for instance, neighbours) and voluntary organisations. The idea of welfare pluralism creates a paradox for community workers. We want communities, in many respects, to take charge of their own welfare, and, in effect, this is what we often work towards in small ways. However, most of us also want to see an extension of welfare. Yet the idea that communities should take charge of their own welfare is mostly advanced by governments which are concerned to spend less on welfare and which expect, in effect, the family to provide more care. Moreover, it is much easier for government to cut funds to voluntary bodies than to fire its own employees, which means that enabling the 'community to care for itself' can become in reality a most exploitative option, and one which is particularly exploitative of women. (See Brenton, 1985, for a detailed discussion of these arguments).

In principle, the answer for a community worker facing such dilemmas is simple; the worker and her colleagues in the agency need to ask themselves whether the proposed programme would be likely to result in a net benefit for the community in both the short and the long term, and, if it would not, to refrain from engaging in it. In practice, however, the choice is often an impossible one: consequences are difficult to predict and so many other factors influence a decision – the need for a voluntary organisation to retain some funding for example.

In Britain, community organisations have, understandably, been slow to enter a particular field: the privatisation of services. Like it or not a range of social services are being privatised, from school meals services to the management of and ownership of council housing estates. While this is sometimes seen as a reactionary kind of conservatism, paradoxically it does offer scope, at least in theory, for community organisations to tender for contracts. In the USA community development corporations (CDSs) often run services for local government and in some cases have budgets of several million dollars. In the process they gain a good deal of business expertise. (See Twelvetrees, 1989, for a discussion of CDCs.) If such services are well run they are usually at least as good as those provided by private firms and indeed by local government, and they offer, in addition, a measure of community empowerment. However, the whole field of community-run services is a complex one and community organisations should not enter it lightly.

In the future community workers and community organisations may increasingly become involved in negotiations with private enterprise. Private firms may become possible sources of funding or they may make key decisions which will affect people's lives. By and large we have little experience and therefore little skill in negotiating with these and related bodies.

There are obviously enormous issues here, which it is not possible to cover in any detail. But the structural changes now occuring in the British welfare state will demand professionals with community work skills and will offer many opportunities as well as pitfalls. We need to think through these issues carefully so that we are prepared to act appropriately when the opportunities arise.

The project planning process

Service professionals are trained to perform at what is ultimately the most important level of an operation, that is, face to face with consumers. Their main concern is not at the planning level. However, in order to ensure that the social worker or teacher (for instance) 'at the sharp end' does her job properly, planning and managerial tasks have to be undertaken. If they are undertaken badly, field staff and, more importantly, the consumers suffer. When one is involved in project-planning and management, one's mental set has to switch from the relatively mono-dimensional focus of the service professional, to the multi-dimensional focus of the planner, who has to take many different requirements into account at the same time. Whether one is establishing a one-evening-a-week advice service staffed by volunteers or a complex scheme employing hundreds or even thousands of staff, whether the project primarily involves a change of policy within one's own agency or whether it means establishing a new organisation, it is necessary to consider a number of points. The first of these is:

Who wants it?

This point is well made by Smiley (1982) in an article about a journey to Abilene. He recounts how all members of his family thought the others wanted to take the trip to Abilene, and did not want to go themselves. However, they only discovered this after a disastrous day out. Setting up projects which nobody wants is very easily done. Somebody suggests 'let's run a carnival' expecting that is what the others in the group want. They don't, but say yes because they think he wants it and will make sure it works. It is always useful to try to work out who wants a particular project and why. Often nobody wants it.

What need will it meet?

If the proposal is, for instance, to run a newsletter, what is it hoped that this will achieve? What will be different from the present situation if the newsletter is established? People often focus on the means rather than on the end. We need to think about ends.

What alternatives are there?

Once there is clarity about the need which is to be met, alternative ways of meeting it should be evaluated. If there are high numbers of isolated elderly people in an area what are alternative ways of reducing their isolation? I can think of about fifty, from setting up a voluntary visiting scheme to compulsorily admitting them all to care! The point of evaluating alternatives is that we often spring into action to run a project in a particular way without thinking about the most effective way of meeting the need.

Who else has tried this and what were the problems?

If we are keen to get involved in a particular project we often go into it because we want it to succeed rather than because there is a likelihood of success. These pitfalls can sometimes be avoided if we discover from other people or from books how such a project can be run, rather than re-inventing the often broken wheel. A related point is:

Will it succeed?

As we wish, presumably, to be involved with successful projects it makes sense to estimate the chances of success. This does not mean that we should only establish projects which are bound to succeed but that most of our projects should have a better than even chance of success.

What resources are required?

Resources include money, plant (for example, vehicles, buildings, reprographic equipment) skilled workers (or volunteers) and time. Where are these resources available? Are they adequate? Can they be obtained in time? Resources are often too few and there is a danger that we will cut our coat to skimpily. In my experience it is usually better to employ one worker on a good salary with adequate backup than try to squeeze two under-resourced workers out of the money available who will soon leave for a better job if they are any good. Similarly, I have found it wisest not to appoint staff about whom one has major doubts because nobody else is available. It is better to re-advertise. Also, most projects take longer to get going than we think. It is important to try to plan the time it will take accurately (then double it!)

Where is the engine?

In any project at least one person has to be determined to make it work. It has to have an engine; somebody who will burn the midnight oil if necessary. If there is no other engine the community worker may need to become the engine or hope, perhaps in vain, that a leader or leaders emerge as the project gets going, which often does not happen.

Obstacles

What is likely to prevent the project succeeding? Does it run counter to a major existing policy? Do certain powerful people have a vested interest in its failure? If so, how can they be converted or bypassed? Resnick and Patti (1980) make some excellent points about the importance of predicting resistance in organisational change and preparing one's response to that resistance. (See also Lauffer, 1978, and Brager and Holloway, 1978.)

It can sometimes take a long time finding out about the institutional obstacles to new projects. Therefore the best prepared community worker is one who familiarises herself as far as possible with the internal politics both of her own organisation and likely target organisations in advance of any project, since she will then have a good eye for spotting both opportunities and potential problems. This takes meticulous work.

A further obstacle can be lack of agency expertise. There is always a slow learning curve for any organisation which starts a new activity, and to run a sophisticated project in an area where the agency has no existing expertise is usually disastrous. Thus, the first profit-making enterprises of social service agencies tend to fail.

Who else should be consulted or involved?

The times when potential supporters can be turned into opponents because we have failed to inform, consult or involve them at an early stage, are without number. In our keenness to get moving we may forget to ask ourselves who else could appropriately be involved. It pays of course to seek to discover whether such people have the power to harm the project before we spend a lot of time seeking to obtain their support.

There may also be persons whom we do not wish to involve, and ways need to be considered of excluding them as neatly as possible.

The need for allies

It is always more difficult to get things done than to do nothing. Doing nothing is safer. So any new project needs allies. But these allies need to be in place well before the project starts, which again underlines the importance of permanent contact making. Allies may sometimes provide inside information which helps our case. Sometimes, however, that information is secret and we cannot use it freely. Otherwise we may compromise our ally. Great care and forethought is necessary in these kinds of situations.

What kind of organisational structure is necessary?

Most new non-statutory projects need constitutions. They may need to register as charities. They may also want to incorporate as a limited liability company. Questions such as the composition and size of the management committee will also need to be considered, and there are often two conflicting needs here. First, effective decisions are best taken by groups of less than ten. But a small group often has to have legitimacy through a wider constituency, which usually means occasional meetings of a large group which, in theory, sets policy. In reality, however, a large group cannot even set policy easily. It depends on how far the small executive group prepares the decisions for the policy-making group to decide about. Another dilemma here is whether to seek legitimacy through having constituent organisations send representatives to the management committee, in which case there is likely to be a lot of dead wood, or to seek out committed and able individuals. A related point is how to be representative in a real rather than a tokenistic way (for instance the all-male white group which then co-opts a token woman or black person). In principle, the way round this is to consider all the interests which should be represented *at the beginning* and to ensure that the invited membership reflects as far as possible the kinds of diversity necessary to be representative and legitimate. But this can take a great deal of time, which is always in short supply.

There is a perennial tension between the need for both participation and decisive action, to which there are no easy solutions. See Holloway and Otto's excellent book *Getting Organized*, 1988, for useful tips about organisation, and *Voluntary but not Amateur*, London Voluntary Service Council (1988), for assistance on constitutional and legal points.

'No' can be a very good answer

After doing careful pre-planning, most of us feel reluctant not to go ahead, even if it looks a high risk project. However, failure at a later stage would be even worse. So it is no disgrace to pull out if feasibility work shows the project is not likely to be viable.

Worker role

Community workers are primarily people who get things going and then move on when the project is successful. This applies to social planning as well as to community development. In getting new projects or services off the ground a worker has again to decide whether to play the role of facilitator and withdraw as soon as she can or whether to play an organising and, later, a managerial role, though there are many combinations of both organising and facilitating roles. The worker's role should be decided in consultation with her supervisor, and, if possible, with the other participants too.

Project implementation

Many of the points relevant to implementing projects have been covered above. The implementation stage is the time we actually get the resources, set up the organisation, rent the building, hire and induct staff and so on. Of these, hiring staff is by far the most important. Working out a systematic procedure for ensuring that, as far as possible, the person who is best for the job gets it pays enormous dividends. Hiring staff is often done without due care.

However, there is only one thing we can really know about the implementation phase, namely, it will throw up unforeseen problems! Therefore, the new venture has to be carefully watched at this stage so that these problems can be sorted out. That is, good feedback mechanisms have to be put into place which will reveal potential problems at an early stage, so they can be corrected before they become serious. It also always pays at this stage to establish an effective administrative filing and accounts system.

Project management

Management is obviously an enormous task and it can only be dealt with briefly here. My own experience of management is in non-statutory agencies and that is the emphasis of this section. However, most of the principles also apply to other settings. Also, I am not, primarily, writing for managers. I am writing for community workers who find themselves in managerial positions, whose way of looking at the world is from the consumer's perspective and who may initially, distrust the idea of management.

The need for an overview

Fieldworkers are usually, quite rightly, effective advocates for their particular client group but may not take the needs of other client groups adequately into account. A project manager has to 'keep her fingers on all the ends'. Agencies also need to develop their work consistently in a particular direction, yet keen professional workers or volunteers may all wish to innovate in different directions at once. They might pay little attention to the fact that the funding was to be reviewed in nine months, and that now is not the appropriate time to be starting high risk new projects for instance.

Agency maintenance

Once a project has been set up it does not run for ever. It may be necessary to renegotiate the resources to run it each year and that may mean adapting the role of the agency slightly to obtain different kinds of funding. Or there may be changes in senior personnel or in the political make-up of the council, which means that the agency's funders need convincing all over again that the project has value. Another important aspect of project maintenance is to ensure that the structure of the agency or organisation remains appropriate to the task or tasks in hand. A voluntary management committee, for example, needs infusions of new blood from time to time and has to find ways of keeping in touch with the staff. Consequently, the manager of a voluntary agency needs to give considerable attention to getting good people onto her management committee.

Agency maintenance covers a wide range of activities, from raising the necessary funding to making sure the staff get their pay cheques (many organisations are very sloppy about this), and from making sure the central heating is working properly to attending the mayor's banquet. Innovatory agencies usually run on a shoestring and operate from inadequate buildings. The overall manager has to ensure that the basic conditions of employment are reasonably adequate. She does not have to undertake these tasks herself – though in an emergency she may have to sweep flood water from the basement, for instance. But she needs to ensure a system is put into place whereby these tasks are undertaken by others.

Many agency staff are excellent fieldworkers but fail to convince important outsiders that they are doing a good job. Effective public relations is, thus, important in virtually all organisations. In statutory agencies it largely means finding ways of ensuring that those in the higher echelons of the organisation know about and appreciate the value of the particular service which is being delivered. In non-statutory organisations, in particular, the emphasis needs to be on showing the wider public, politicians and potential funding agencies the value of the work. It can mean regular well produced reports, press releases, open days, talks to other organisations and the like.

A sense of strategy

'What business are we in?' has to be the permanent question which managers ask themselves. This kind of strategising leads to decisions which influence the direction taken by the organisation. As a university lecturer, I once spent a good deal of time involved in local projects. I later considered this and thought that it would be a more appropriate use of my time to develop short courses for practitioners, which I did.

That is an example of an individual strategic decision. But such decisions need primarily to be made at the agency level. This obviously requires consultation but, once the strategy has been decided, it is often the manager who has to ensure that the policy is adhered to. However, a strategy to concentrate on one area, by definition, means that other areas must be neglected unless a case is made out that these should now take priority.

Financial planning and work planning

Strategic planning merges with financial and work planning. The days have passed when community workers went out and 'did their own thing'. But most agencies still do not plan their work effectively. Ideally, each particular activity needs to be planned in terms of worker hours necessary per week. There should also, of course, be a budget and a running check should be kept on expenditure on a monthly basis in order to monitor it.

Similarly, the sequence of actions in a project needs to be properly worked out. In the case of conferences, for instance, the venue needs to be booked before publicity material is issued. Enough advance notice also needs to be given, for instance, for delegates to apply to their agencies for funding. These and similar points need to be taken account of when setting the date, otherwise time can run out.

Much of industry follows work plans where the year's objectives, calculated on a realistic basis, are spelt out on paper in advance so that checks can easily be made as to whether targets are being reached. Some welfare organisations are now trying to do this, and, while forward planning of this nature could be taken to extremes, I believe that community workers, if they are to be effective, need to adopt some of these practices too.

At a more basic level still, day to day work needs to be planned properly. How many staff meetings have you gone to where no record is kept of important decisions, or somebody has come with a good but not well thought out idea which has been discussed for an hour before people realise the matter has to be deferred to the next meeting so that more work can be done on it beforehand? In how many organisations does the chair not know what she is supposed to be doing? How often is there an argument about what decision the previous meeting actually reached? Similarly, how often have you taken part in a meeting without being clear why and what you want? When we are pressed, even thirty seconds' thought about our objectives in advance of the meeting can help.

Community workers also often find themselves on the management committees of organisations they set up, the main purpose of which is to set policy, hire senior staff and perhaps to play a part in agency maintenence. Yet we are not usually very knowledgeable about these managerial responsibilities.

People management

One thing stands out in people management, namely that the greater the sense of ownership which the staff (including volunteers) in an organisation develop the greater the commitment and the more effective their work will be. Closely related to this is the vital need we all have to be recognised.

A major task of a manager is to resource her staff. Part of this is ensuring that they work in reasonable conditions. Another part is being available when they want advice. A lot of it is valuing them and their work, giving them the space to take risks, to make mistakes, knowing when to offer help, being concerned about their long term development, even when this will take them out of the agency, utilising their talents, listening to their ideas.

For many community workers this is the only side of staff management which we value, since we associate top down authoritarianism with the word management. There is, however, another consideration, which I call quality control.

A senior community worker was supervising and resourcing several less experienced workers in the ways mentioned above. However the reports one of them was providing about his work with groups seemed a bit odd. So she checked up, to find that he had not been near the groups for weeks and had been fabricating his records. This is an extreme example oɪ poor work. There are many more which are less extreme. Some of us are slow at writing reports. Others of us regularly manage to annoy our colleagues. Yet others fail to plan with sufficient attention to detail. It is ultimately the responsibility of the manager to ensure that the service to the consumer is as effective as possible, and this includes helping staff improve their performance.

Thus, the sometimes difficult task of the manager is to combine the resourcing with the quality control aspects of managing.

Increasingly, effective organisations also review the performance of all staff on a regular basis. This is, in my view, an essential staff development procedure and should not be confused with discipline. Holloway and Otto (1985, p. 26) have produced some useful guidelines on this. However, that somewhat bureaucratic approach has also to be tempered with what, according to Peters and Waterman (1982) and Peters and Austin (1985) makes for successful organisations, namely:

(a) valuing staff;
(b) being passionately concerned that the customers (con-
     sumers) are satisfied, and that staff adhere to central
     values such as the vital importance of good customer
     service;
(c) constant innovation and entrepreneurship;
(d) good leadership; and
(e) 'management by wandering about' (that is by ensuring
     that there is considerable informal face to face contact
     between managers and staff).

While these attributes emerged from studies of successful companies many of them would equally well apply to successful social welfare organisations.

Managing volunteers

There are many different kinds of volunteer. However, in this section I am referring to voluntary work in the more usual sense of the word, where the volunteer works under the auspices of an agency. My frame of reference is also now neighbourhood community work where the volunteers may be from outside the locality and may well also be of a different class and culture from residents.

Some community groups with which a worker is in contact require particular services which neither she nor other members of the community are able to provide. For instance, many members of the disabled club with which I worked required help with shopping and transport. There may also be projects which a worker wishes to initiate, such as a youth club, which no local people seem able or willing to take on. If it is done sensitively, volunteers from another locality and of a different social class can be usefully involved in many community activities.

If volunteers are needed for complex and responsible tasks, like running a playgroup, it is necessary to spend a good deal of time helping them to think through the implications of the work, the stress it may place on them, for example. For some activities, especially those to do with children, it may be important to take up references and to make thorough enquiries about their suitability. In these kinds of situations it will usually be necessary to exercise some control over the volunteers when they start, since the scope for misunderstanding and possible conflict between volunteer and residents is too great for the worker not to keep a careful watch on the situation. Unless a worker spends a considerable amount of time with volunteers before they start work, during which she will also be assessing which kind of activity would be most suitable for them, she may wish to give them simple tasks first, like delivering a newsletter, after which they can be moved on to more difficult tasks. We must be careful here though. To be given an over-simple task can seem like an insult. As many volunteers leave because they are underused or are given only vague tasks as leave because they are overworked. We also need to consider how to provide continuing support. This can sometimes be done satisfactorily through a regular support group. A few really good volunteers may eventually become colleagues who develop and manage their own area of interest without a great deal of supervision or support.

Local activists as paid community workers?

Many projects employ local people often on a part-time basis, and this is one of the strengths of community work. There are dangers however, and it is on these that I wish to concentrate by giving two examples, the second concerning a case where it went badly wrong. Grace, a local resident, carried out a great deal of advice work in her own home. When she had been associated with our project for about five years we began paying her to run one or two sessions in our advice centre. These sessions gradually increased and after another three years we employed her full-time. This was the length of time she needed in order to build up her confidence and become accustomed to the ethos and the many unwritten customs of a professional social work agency.

Jack, the leader of the adventure playground had a voluntary helper, Greg. But Greg was not particularly liked by the children, and was obviously meeting his own needs rather than those of the children. When money became available for a second playleader, Greg applied and Jack did not discourage him. But there was no way the committee could have appointed him and he did not get the job. He was not prepared for this and caused a great disturbance for some weeks, physically assaulting Jack who had to close the playground for a time and ban Greg from it as a consequence. It is difficult to say what the playleader should have told Greg when he wanted to apply for the job. Perhaps he should have said that Greg could apply, pointing out that there would be other candidates too and there was no guarantee he would get the job. Well worked out hiring procedures should also have helped.

When local activists become employed as community workers they bring a great deal to the work. But because they have lived in the locality for many years they may have a rather rigid and subjective view of the situation. They will have local enemies, as well as friends and useful contacts. The community activist may be an excellent voluntary worker, but as an unpaid worker she could play to her strengths and conceal her weaknesses. Professionals have to work on projects which they may find uncongenial and for which they have little aptitude.

If the community activist is to be employed as a community worker, she needs to learn to become an enabler rather than a leader, and to develop analytical and interactional skills. This jump is not usually easy to make, and it takes time, training and continuing support. While community work consists of transferring skills and confidence to other people and is not a closed profession such as the law, the business of transferring these skills is a high skill in itself. We are not doing anybody any favours if we pretend that these 'facilitating' skills are common currency, and particularly if we employ 'community' people who cannot do the job. However, there are now some 'access' community work courses which acknowledge both the need for and the problems with assisting 'community' people to become paid workers, which seems to me to be the right way to go about providing opportunities for local people to become community workers.

Local management?

Some community workers consider that to be employed directly by a community group is the ideal form of employment, since one is accountable directly to the people with whom one is working. In my experience the reality is rather different. If we consider the nature of community groups – that they tend to be short-lived, have difficulty in managing money, do not always take decisions well and may have a conservative leadership which is easily threatened – it is not surprising that they often lack the ability to manage a professional worker. If a worker is employed by a community group she may get no guidance, she may have to support the group rather than get support and guidance from it. She may not get paid regularly and may even have to work out her own salary and national insurance contributions. A community group may also become over-directive, particularly if the work experience of the members is in employment which has an authoritarian style of management. The worker may not be allowed to work with organisations in the locality with which her employers are not in sympathy, for example. The idea of local management is important and should not be rejected because it has not always worked, but it needs to be carefully thought about.

Supervising professional community workers

In my view, in order to resource professional community workers effectively, to enable them to continue to develop their skills, and to ensure that they work on their areas of weakness, regular supervision is necessary. If two or more workers are working on the same project it can be useful, sometimes, to undertake this together. Nevertheless, while supervision certainly needs to be undertaken in the context of an agency strategy which is likely to have been worked out to some extent collectively, the supervision is essentially individual. An effective community worker plans her work in advance, agrees those plans with her supervisor, monitors and evaluates how far it has been possible to achieve planned objectives and modifies the plan accordingly. In order to be accountable to an agency these plans and their consequences have to be written down as retrievable records. But it is difficult to plan and evaluate alone. Inexperienced workers, especially, require experienced supervisors who can provide 'critical support', and in my view staff need to know that they are going to be held accountable. Thus, meetings with the supervisor will usually cover the work undertaken in the previous month or so and an evaluation of it, plans for future work, the allocation of priorities, and any problems the worker may be facing. With new employees, students on placement and at times of staff reviews the emphasis needs to be on what the worker has learned, what she thinks she does well, and less well, what new areas of knowledge and skill she thinks she needs to gain, and how these objectives can be reached. It also needs to include an opportunity for the worker to comment on the support offered by the supervisor and the agency.

The personal dimension to supervision can be difficult because it relates to individual qualities, such as perseverance, tolerance, and so on. A supervisor is, in my view, avoiding the responsibility of doing her job properly if she studiously avoids the 'personal', but on the other hand she has to be careful not to overstep the boundary between that part of the personal which relates to professional effectiveness and the entirely private concerns of the member of staff. Thus, I usually ask the person I am supervising to determine the agenda. This gives her the space to raise issues which are of concern to her and, often, gives me an opportunity, later, to add my own view. One has to bear in mind, however, that many of us are quite sensitive to a hint of criticism, and one has to be extremely careful how one discusses areas which may be sensitive.

A different view would be that, as long as the person's work is broadly satisfactory the supervisor should not raise anything negative unless asked by the worker.

Most community workers new to project management do not expect to have to discipline or fire staff. Yet it is occasionally necessary. This is why all staff need to know that each organisation has rules and expectations about the quality of work, and that, in the event that this is unsatisfactory, steps will be taken to ensure that a worker performs appropriately or, eventually, leaves. Thus, hiring and firing policies are necessary. If a worker has been getting appropriate supervision, but her work is still unsatisfactory steps need to be taken in accordance with this policy. However, the first step has to be to point out exactly what is not adequate, to indicate what an adequate performance would consist of, and how it would be measured, to try to get the worker to agree to this, and to agree, further, on steps to take which will improve worker performance.

Project evaluation

In many respects, project evaluation is the other side of project planning. Ideally, evaluation has to start with the planning process, the adoption of clear goals, and the identification of what would constitute the attainment of those goals. That is, one needs to be able to say what would and would not be a successful outcome.

Often in community work the goals are almost *i*
measure. Therefore one has to select outcomes *'*
measured but which approximate as closely as p⌐⌐
desired goal. For instance, a volunteer visiting proj⌐⌐
designed to decrease the loneliness of elderly people could
not easily be evaluated. If, however, interviews with the
elderly people who were being visited resulted in a high
proportion of them expressing satisfaction (or dissatisfaction)
with their volunteer, or if several elderly people were
applying of their own volition for such a volunteer then these
'surrogate' measures could be regarded as a fairly accurate
indication of the effectiveness of the scheme. However, good
evaluation research really requires comparative studies
where the changes in a group receiving service are compared
either with the same group before the service started or with a
control group with similar characteristics which did not
receive the service, or both.

Evaluation which is concerned with measuring concrete
outcomes specified in advance is often referred to as the
'goals model'. However, to apply this goals model to
community projects it is often necessary to undertake a good
deal of preliminary work with the organisation. The
researcher may need to help the staff identify what the goals
are and to develop the means to measure whether those goals
have been achieved before undertaking the evaluation.

Another method I have used is to evaluate the organisational strength of an organisation. It is based on the idea that
if the organisation is strong it will be able to 'self correct'. My
assumption would be that if the organisation is ineffective
certain characteristics would obtain, including lack of clear
policies, disagreements among staff about the work to be
done, decisions being taken and not followed through, lack of
involvement of consumers or junior staff in planning, poor
filing and record keeping, confused staff roles, inadequate
support and supervision of staff, lack of clear objectives both
for the organisation as a whole and for individual staff,
considerable criticism from other organisations, and so on. If
these organisational weaknesses are found and are remedied
the organisation is thus in a good position to identify its own
problems and become effective.

Yet another form of evaluation is suitable to organisations with a variety of conflicting goals, or somewhat indefinable goals. Armstrong *et al.* (1976) refer to this as 'critical appraisal'. I once used this method to evaluate some community controlled corporations in the USA which were aimng to promote economic development in deprived areas. I found that the organisations were indeed able to promote economic development but not in deprived areas. Moreover in order to promote it, the community control of the organisation had to be weakened. Thus, the meeting of one goal was at the expense of another. To take another example, the goals of probationers and probation officers may be very different, which makes evaluating outcomes difficult. In addition, many community projects have unanticipated outcomes which also need taking into account.

To evaluate these kinds of projects it is necessary to use a combination of approaches: case studies, studying statistics produced by the organisation, examining records and reports, listing outcomes of the work, interviewing managers, staff, consumers, funders and other agencies in contact with the organisation, in addition to the 'goals method'. Then one has to put the information together and try to form a coherent picture of the effectiveness of the organisation. In doing this it is important not to ignore information which does not fit with the view which usually begins to emerge early on in the process in one's own head about what one would like to be able to conclude! Often research like this results in paradoxical or ambiguous conclusions, for example that certain objectives can only be achieved at the expense of others.

Evaluation needs to be distinguished from 'monitoring'. Monitoring the work of an organisation involves collecting quantified information on a day to day basis to indicate what is being done – number of client contacts, numbers and types of groups worked with, the kinds of resources provided to the groups etc. The types of data gathered would also be determined by the requirements of an evaluation proper, the success of which, would, in turn depend upon the acuracy and relevance of the data obtained in the monitoring process.

Most welfare organisations do not engage in formal

evaluations. But, as I suggest elsewhere, I believe they need to be a bit more precise about planning their objectives so that reasonably objective evaluation becomes more possible. In this process the most important question is 'What, with hindsight, would we do differently?' Thus, one is learning the lessons for future action. A reasonably easy to read summary of the different approaches to evaluation is *Evaluation in the Voluntary Sector* (Ball, 1988).

Politics, power and social planning

Social planning in community work is often regarded as a consensus activity. But that is far from reality. It is highly political and depends on a skilful ability to manipulate the political process. It involves lobbying, political manoeuvering, bargaining and the like.

I think that the politics of power is largely misunderstood by community workers. If one is the director of a large organisation one has, in theory, the power to deploy its resources how one wants, though this power is usually very limited in practice. Community workers are, however, usually in a position of wanting to attract resources for the schemes *they* wish to promote. Thus, we often find ourselves making applications and seeking to *persuade* resource holders that what we want to do is 'a good thing'. This can work. More important however is the ability to discover the self interest of those resource holders. What is it *they* want? They have to deploy their resources somehow, and if we can find ways of giving them what they want, helping them deploy their resources to meet the needs *they* identify, we may be in business. I once had discussions with a governmental agency which was funding my organisation about providing resources for further projects. They said they wanted to see how the existing projects went first. So I suggested they provide resources to evaluate them. Similarly, when a local authority chief executive asked my advice about how his authority should relate to the voluntary sector, which was funded on a very haphazard basis, I said that in my view he should first of all seek to work out a policy towards the voluntary sector, in which we could help if he wished. Thus, I was trying to help him with his problem, not asking him to give me something I wanted.

Another way of securing political support is to seek to ensure that one's political competitors sit on one's own management committee. Usually, in time, they also develop some allegiance to one's own organisation. One has to be careful about this though, since if they are totally opposed to one's organisation they will just cause trouble.

Another means of building power is to assist others to get what they want. Politicians sometimes want to sit on particular community committees for instance. If the worker can arrange this the councillors might turn out to be helpful later on. However, one has to be very careful if one starts to work in this way, since it is a great temptation to build power for one's own ends rather than in order to meet community need. Nevertheless I am convinced that building power consists primarily of identifying the self interest of others and trying to meet that self interest. There has to be some gain in a transaction for all the players; otherwise they will not play.

The other dimension of power which community workers need to be aware of is the need to get issues on political agendas. There may be no chance of getting the resources to run the projects we want to run at a particular stage. But there are usually ways of getting issues on important agendas. For instance, when I wanted to get local authorities in Wales to begin discussing community development I established a relationship with the director of the relevant association of local authorities, and later asked his organisation to co-sponsor a conference on the subject. Without his assistance I would not have been able to attract local authorities.

Social planning and personal change

The literature about organisational change recognises forms of resistance to change rooted in individual personalities (for example, conservers, climbers, professionals (Resnick and Patti, 1980). The literature of community work emphasises the importance of consciousness raising and personal change in community groups, recognising that structural change must be accompanied by personal change. Community workers also need to think about how to encourage the necessary personal change in the service delivery and policy making systems which we seek to influence. This is difficult to do because the worker is not usually engaged as a professional adviser to service providers and does not have the authority to intervene in interpersonal matters at that level. One community worker once attempted this within a relatively benign social service agency. He interviewed the main service providers about a particular project, and later summarised what they said and fed it back to them in a synthesised form, as a result of which some of them modified their practice. I cannot make specific suggestions as to how attitude change in service providers can be brought about. But I believe that it is as important as structural change and that community workers need to give considerable attention to this.

6
Community Work and Social Change

Working the system

Specht (1975) has identified four broad 'modes of intervention' in relation to promoting social change; collaboration, campaign, contest and violence, with particular sets of tactics applying to each.

A collaborative approach (which can also be called working the system) is applicable when there is consensus about the issue between, let us say, the community group and the local authority, or the staff of an organisation and its management. Here, the action group does research, writes reports, sets up joint working parties with people in the target system and negotiates a changed procedure, not without disagreement and the use of power, but the power of argument, good presentation and, if necessary, the influence of allies.

Even in collaborative work timing is of the essence, and it is also necessary to seek out friends within the system one wishes to change, who can advise one when the time is ripe to act. A worker needs the help of these contacts to use their influence in converting other people to her cause and to leak information. It is also important to find the 'right way in'. A community organisation had been trying to contact the leader of the council. I discovered that a contact of mine was on close terms with the leader and I asked him to set up an informal meeting. As a result the group received a more sympathetic hearing than if they had written a letter because the town clerk would probably have prevented the matter from being presented to the leader in the way the group wanted.

In order to bring influence to bear on any organisation either from the inside or the outside, a worker needs to build up an alliance, starting probably with her closest colleagues,

140

and gradually converting more people inside and outside the organisation. She needs to know particularly who her enemies are, and to try to win as many other people as possible over to her side, so that her opponents will have no support. She must prepare her argument carefully and must use the device of the report – the instrument which bureaucracies use par excellence as one means of bringing about change. A chief officer once told me how the housing committee had made a 'daft decision' (his words). His reaction was to write a report pointing this out, and he got it changed at the next committee. A sound principle to follow is that it is best to bring pressure on the target from as many different sources as possible: other field workers, politicians, unions, professional organisations, consumer groups, central government and particularly from any source which has real power to influence the situation. But unless workers are in an overt fight with their organisation that pressure has to be subtle, and they need to be careful how far they go in allowing their superiors to find out that they have caused another organisation to pressurise their employers. It is also important not to over-estimate one's support. The forces of reaction are usually more powerful than the forces for change.

If the leader of the Conservative Party says that nationalisation has failed, we might argue that such a view from such a source is predictable. But if someone on the left of the Labour Party says so, we think again. The irony is that 'progressive' ideas are more likely to be listened to if they come from someone who is seen as conservative than if they come from someone with a more radical image (see Resnick, 1975, p. 465). For this reason it is necessary to find the right people to present the group's arguments to those people who are likely to be most resistant. Thus, negotiating strategies and tactics must be planned in detail and rehearsed with the negotiating group in order to predict how the other side will react.

The advantage of working within the system is that a worker has greater access to information. She may also have access to influential contacts, although some departmental hierarchies prevent this. But she should know how her own department works, its sensitive points and how it is likely to react. There is no substitute for this knowledge. However, she is bound by the limitations her own agency imposes and, since she carries to some degree its reputation, she may also use only a limited range of tactics. Open conflict will not be tolerated, so she has to be very canny. A student on placement with the housing department asked the housing manager to attend a public meeting, which he refused. I advised the student to talk quietly with a councillor with whom he already had some contact. He did and as a result the housing manager was told to attend the meeting by the councillors!

Once the change the group of the worker wants has been approved it must be structured into the routine of the organisation. The worker must make sure that it becomes agreed policy, that adequate resources are devoted to it, and that staff are in post whose responsibility it is to operate the new procedure. Initally, however, the worker might have to perform a 'watchdog' function to ensure that the system did not revert to old ways of operating. Whatever we are engaged in, the most important attribute is the *will* to make it work. The majority of people 'tread water', they respond to what comes at them but they do not initiate. If one is working with a community group, running a campaign, or even in charge of a major department, one usually finds that most other people work in this reactive rather than pro-active way. To bring about change a worker must personally ensure that the necessary tasks get done. The test of a good organiser, politician or leader, is whether she is content merely to go through the motions of changing the situation by sitting in endless committees which do nothing but talk, or whether she will personally concern herself with enough aspects of the process to ensure that change happens.

Working the system never gets us *all* we want. It also involves compromise and incremental gains. It is a slow process which requires the ability to see and exploit opportunities within a constantly changing political environment. But there are always opportunities which an entrepreneurial community worker can take advantage of who is prepared to work in this way.

When a worker is working within the system for change she has to be aware of the danger of being exploited. The system may find ways of adapting to pressure without changing for the better. She may become so conscious of the constraints that she is afraid to test out the imagined limits because everyone is scared of upsetting a particular politician. She can also get 'sucked in' by the common and pervasive feeling within large public service organisations that it is so difficult to improve the situation that it is not worth bothering. Or she may become so immersed in day to day 'wheeler dealing' to achieve minor objectives that she loses sight of strategic goals. Nevertheless, if there is, broadly speaking, issue consensus between the various partners involved it makes most sense to try to bring about change through this kind of collaborative approach.

Campaigns and contests

When the two parties involved in an issue have different views about how the matter should be resolved (issue difference) but the one party still recognises the legitimacy of the other party to decide on the matter (a motorway proposal, the allocation of resources for a community centre, the cleaning up of an eyesore for instance) the most appropriate form of action is a campaign.

In practice, campaigning merges at one end with collaboration and at the other with contest. A worker or group involved in an influence strategy may well commence with a collaborative approach and, when it is not successful, move through campaigning to contest. If the contest is won, then it is necessary in most situations for collaborative relationships to be established once again. However any one strategy may also require collaborative, campaign and contest work at the same time, which should preferably be undertaken by different people.

Walton (1976) makes this point well where he contrasts a collaborative influence strategy, which he calls an 'attitude change' strategy, with a contest, or in his terms, a 'power' strategy. A power strategy (sometimes called the social action model of community work) seeks to expose, embarrass and discredit the other side and to polarise the issue in order to build the power of one's own organisation and force the opponents to concede. It involves strikes, boycotts, sit-ins, disruptive tactics and the skilful use of the media. On the other hand, the attitude change approach involves establishing close relationships with the other side, empathising with their view of the situation, minimising differences, sharing information, building trust and making attempts to solve the problem jointly.

A major consideration, if a worker or a community group is involved in a campaign or contest, is whether a powerful enough organisation can be built both to force the opponent to concede and to sustain the victory. If so, it matters less that the group may be alienating its opponents, and even some people who might otherwise have been neutral, by the methods used. I am thinking particularly of disruptive tactics such as heckling during council meetings, take-overs, sit-ins and obstructive demonstrations. However, if the group is campaigning on one issue, but has a useful co-operative relationship with the authorities in other areas, disruptive tactics may jeopardise that relationship. More importantly, if the community organisation is unable to build the power to coerce the other side successfully, which is by far the most common situation, then the members need to think carefully about how far to provoke that opponent, and whether care should be taken not to alienate its representatives, in which case non-militant rather than militant tactics may have to be used. I am surprised how often community workers do not think these issues through.

Experienced campaigners (Bryant, 1979; Bryant and Bryant, 1982; and Alinsky, 1972) give great attention to the importance of building a strong organisation before engaging in confrontation. Alinsky would not even go into an area until he was invited by an organisation representing the community which would guarantee an adequate sum of money for his team to do their work. Consequently he began with an established organisation and with secure and independent funding. Few workers in Britain are financed independently. Directly or indirectly most funds come from the state, which makes confrontation difficult. Alinsky mentions a range of tactics which can be used, such as provoking the opponent so that he brings himself down by his own reaction. But if a group is not properly prepared the opponent will bring the group down by that reaction. Alinsky's statement sums it up well, ' "Power comes out of the barrel of a gun!" is an absurd rallying cry when the other side has all the guns' (1972, p. xx). See also Wilson (1984) for some useful hints about campaigning in Britain, and in particular his dictum that the campaigner needs to become an expert on the issue in question.

Some of the main points which need to be borne in mind in campaign situations are as follows. First, contests between community groups and other organisations are exercises in guerilla warfare. If you are likely to lose in a straight battle you do not fight but build support behind the scenes and begin to get the issue of concern on relevant agendas. You only come into the open when you stand a good chance of winning. Second, you understand as fully as you can how the opposition works: who are the most powerful people, who has influence on them, and how they will react to a particular strategy or tactic on your part. You need to think about whether you are in a situation where both sides stand to win something, in which case you may be able to persuade the other side without a confrontation of the superiority of your case, or whether you are in a situation where if you win they must lose, or vice versa. In the latter case, an approach based on persuasion probably stands little chance and coercion may be needed, though if the group cannot build enough power it will lose.

In the campaign which is an exercise in coercion, some of the tactics you use will be confrontational and disruptive, which have the aim of embarrassing the authorities and attracting the attention of the media. But the disruption should only be one tactic within a broader strategy containing a range of different tactics. Once the council chamber has been occupied a few times it begins to lose its force and one needs to consider other methods: petitions, a continuing barrage of letters, processions which are likely to attract the media because they contain tableaux depicting the issue in question, for example. Vary your tactics, take the opposition by surprise, and keep the initiative. Even when involved in confrontation the battle of ideas still needs to be fought, however, and every opportunity must be taken to present well-researched argument, using experts when appropriate.

When it comes to negotiation with the opposition, a group needs to be clear about its negotiating strategy. In the first negotiation you may be frightened and unsure, and so will the members of your group. If you are trying to help *them* to negotiate rather than doing it yourself, you will have to spend many hours preparing them in great detail. For instance, one community worker I knew took some tenants the previous day to the rather plush committee room in which the negotiation was to take place, so that they would not be over-awed by their surroundings. Remember too that 'the other side' are likely to feel nervous. They may also be inexperienced, and there may be ways of exploiting this.

Battles between organisations are largely fought at long range with each side preparing its tactics with care. Although a hastily planned demonstration executed while people *feel* like fighting can sometimes win the day, mostly it does not. While the hearts of people have to be engaged in what they are doing their actions must be thought out. If the group's representatives are too worked up they may well miss an opportunity to make important points in a negotiation or a confrontation.

Some writers say that a campaign should be rewarding in some way. Well, of course it should, but that is a tall order. There is no way that all the preparation, the organisation-building, the letter-writing, the waiting, can be enjoyable all the time. Mainly it is hard work. However, an effective community worker also gives attention to making the work fun for the participants. The North Americans, in particular, seem very good at this, by ending serious meetings with the joint singing of an old civil rights song, for instance.

Towards a radical practice?

The above influence strategies could be used to achieve either progressive or reactionary objectives. They are more or less value neutral. But there are other approaches.

For over a decade the radical tendency in British community work has struggled to apply what can now be seen as a socialist/feminist analysis of society to the practice of community work. That is, they have tried to find ways of doing work which, instead of reinforcing the current (capitalist) system, are not only instrumental in moving towards a radically different society but which also 'prefigure' what that society would look like in the approaches which are taken.

Hatton, an experienced community worker in Cardiff whose roots are in the radical tendency, seeks to adopt the following principles in his work.

(1) Freire's ideas of establishing an authentic dialogue with the members of the communities with which one is working, based on how they see their world.
(2) Marxian ideas about the nature of welfare (namely that while the welfare state exists, in the last analysis, to enhance the development of the capitalist system, the contradictions within capitalism provide space for working class people (and other oppressed groups) to exploit the system to obtain real benefits).
(3) The tactics developed by Alinsky.
(4) Ideas to do with mutually supportive ways of working developed by the Women's Movement.

For him a successful community action must:

(a) resolve the particular problem, such as getting the pavements repaired;
(b) involve ways of working in which people can become more aware;
(c) involve democratic ways of working;
(d) involve a link with broader social change.

He considers that political theory, while vitally important to give a long term sense of direction can, if one is not careful, over-influence the way one works so that one neglects what people actually want in favour of longer term objectives. He emphasises the need for socialists to be much more aware of what they are trying to do, and, for instance, to discover how political structures work in order to influence them. 'We need to understand local authority practices and that, for example, there is often an underspend at the end of the year. Previously we just created a fuss!'

In his view, opposition is not sufficient alone. It is necessary to have created a vision. Thus, in some work he did with claimants on welfare rights he ensured that time was spent discussing what a good income maintenance system would look like. He is also hopeful that the development of good links with unions could result in their funding certain aspects of community action. However, he has found that it pays to remain independent of political parties and trades unions, while having good links with them, because it is easy to get drawn into their concerns. He took the view that an attempt to get the director of social services to implement a welfare benefits take up campaign in which he was involved was successful because the action group was independent of a political party. (Taken from a lecture by Hatton, 1988).

Burghardt (1981), writing from a Marxist perspective, is concerned that radicals give general prescriptions for practice without saying what the worker should actually do and how to do it. Drawing heavily on Freire (1978) but also on Rogers (1961) he emphasises that, in all social work (including community work) the personal has to be emphasised as well as the political, that workers have to listen to the people with whom they are working, that they have to recognise their own weaknesses, that they must be prepared to challenge the people with whom they are working and really engage with them. This also involves many of the skills associated both with assertiveness and with Rogerian counselling. Burghardt is particularly interesting on non-racist and sexist work in that he suggests that a worker can reach a state of empathy with the individuals with whom he is working by consciously thinking about situations in which he has felt oppressed or excluded.

The kind of engagement which Burghardt favours is based on the worker accepting and acknowledging her own weaknesses. On top of this she must want to understand the view that the people she works with have of the world (getting them to 'name their world' – Freire) and she must take it seriously (which can mean arguing with them in a dialogical process). Only then, Burghardt suggests, does the critical process of action-reflection-action really start happening because the worker is relating as an equal, or co-worker in the process of growth, which encompasses both instrumental and personal change. If the worker does not become involved in this way she is just using the members of the community as cannon fodder because they are not involved in a process of growth.

To work in this way requires a great deal of inner strength, as well as practice and careful supervision, at least initially. It requires those of us with the Achilles' heel of many welfare workers, namely, the fear of upsetting people, to get beyond that fear, as we learn to act in ways which are challenging yet based on empathy and humility.

It must be remembered that meaningful personal change is extraordinarily painful (for all of us) a point which Burghardt makes several times, as we move from one set of assumptions about ourselves and the world to another. Like Burghardt, I find that ideas drawn from transactional analysis (see Harris, 1985) assertiveness training, humanistic psychology (see for example, Rowe, 1987) counselling theory (Rogers, 1961) have helped me begin to become a subject of my own actions rather than an object of other people's actions (Freire, 1978). I think they are a set of tools, which, whatever our political perspective, can give us the belief in ourselves, the courage and the technical skills necessary to assist other people to make what Thomas (1978) calls the 'Journey into the Acting Community'.

In her intellectually honest article ('Recapturing Sisterhood: A critical look at "process" in feminist organising and community work', 1980) Barker carefully and critically analyses the application to community work of a number of principles developed by the Women's Liberation Movement (WLM). In particular she looks at the idea that a female community worker should minimise the differences between herself and the women with whom she is working, underplay her own expertise, share her own personal concerns with the group, encourage the formation of an unstructured group to facilitate participation and so on. Barker is of the opinion that it is possible to fall into a 'false equality' trap and, in effect patronise the people with whom one is working. She concludes that differences must be honestly acknowledged in an atmosphere of mutual respect.

I think that some of the principles which are being developed by the WLM and others about how to help the people we work with act upon the world and grow at the same time are central to the development of new forms of practice. But I am equally sure that making them work requires the intellectual honesty and personal courage shown by Barker and Burghardt.

Racism, sexism and the other 'isms

Ohri, Manning and Curno (1982) offer the following guidelines to white workers about how to work in non-racist ways (I summarise):

(1)   recognise that racism is a reality throughout British society;
(2)   understand that racism is a white problem;
(3)   *all of us* need to find non-racist ways of working;
(4)   recognise that you collude with racism;
(5)   monitor whether the group or organisation in which you are involved is acting in a racist way;
(6)   your primary role is to challenge white racism (supporting black self help is secondary);
(7)   do not confuse having relationships with black people with anti-racism;
(8)   encourage other workers to work together to combat racism;
(9)   familiarise yourself with issues of concern to the black community.

Many of these precepts could apply equally well to ageism, for instance.

There is, however, no prescription for working in non-sexist, ageist or racist ways. It is, in my view, a matter of awareness, self monitoring, particularly of our assumptions (are we surprised when we find a female senior citizen as chair of the housing committee, for instance?), the language we use, and finding the courage to assert values to do with empowering people in disadvantaged positions, and of incorporating into our practice some of the ways of engaging with people expounded by Burghardt. Opportunities to challenge (for instance) sexist behaviour continually arise. In a discussion between three community workers about information technology one (a woman) kept putting herself down saying that she could not easily cope with it. Her colleague who was showing off his knowledge about computer systems remarked jokingly that, as she was a woman she would not understand these things. The third worker, an expert in this field, challenged this by saying that he did not like the suggestion that because she was a woman the other worker could not easily come to grips with information technology. But he also pointed out that she was in fact asking the right questions though she did not have the specific terminology. Thus he challenged what he perceived as sexist behaviour but validated the 'victim' at the same time.

There are also many equal opportunity and affirmative action policies which we need to ensure are adopted by the organisations we work in. It is particularly important to try to ensure that the appropriate tone is set at the top.

Broad-based organising

We saw above that none of the approaches developed so far, by either the professional or the radical tendency in community work has brought about major structural change. We have also seen that many community organisations are not successful in achieving their stated goals and often collapse whether they win or lose. There is no community movement of relatively disadvantaged people to compare, for example, with trades unions. Moreover, there has been a growing recognition that community workers have to find better ways of developing people rather than using them as cannon fodder in the latest campaign. It is observable too that successful community groups often oppress more needy groups, homeless people for instance. Community groups also tend to be reactive – they try to stop a motorway – rather than being pro-active; getting involved in the planning of an effective and cheap transportation system.

In recognition of these and other aspects of the failure of citizen action the Industrial Areas Foundation (IAF) in the USA has developed an effective form of 'broad based' organising which works in the following way.

The IAF supplies an organiser to set up an organisation in a large 'neighbourhood' (for example, East Brooklyn, south central Los Angeles) at the request of an independent sponsoring committee (which the IAF may well have helped to set up), but only after the sponsoring committee has raised enough money to employ the organiser for three years. The organiser identifies persons in the community who are:

(a)   committed to building an organisation representing all the community's interests (that is who are not concerned merely with one issue, for instance housing); and who are

(b)   committed to democratic and 'Judaeo-Christian' values (who often turn out to be clergy, professionals and lower middle class people).

The organiser then sets about training these leaders and building the organisation. However, it has been found that the quickest way to do this is to make it an organisation of organisations, primarily church organisations, because these have fewer vested interests than other organisations, which then pay dues to the central organisation.

The aim of an organiser is to build a powerful organisation explicitly based on the self interest of the members. The organisation, once established, uses that power to get into relationship with major power-holders, senior politicians, company presidents etc, a relationship which is then used to get into relationship with other power-holders and to ensure that policies are changed in order to benefit the neighbourhood in question. However, real power is only generated through the respect of equals. Therefore, the community organisation has to build its power through research and the careful and disciplined organisation of large numbers of people. If hundreds, or, in some cases, thousands of people are assembled for an 'action' (public meeting) where the target is the Mayor of New York the press will be present (and they have always been carefully briefed) and if the demands of the organisation have been carefully researched and are realistic the power of the mass organisation together with the media constitute a considerable pressure on the Mayor to bring about major change.

Actions are kept short. Committee members agree to bring quotas of followers (and are held to account in the evaluation if they do not bring their quota). Issues are chosen which will unify the organisation rather than divide it, which will politicise the community and which the target can agree to. For instance, Mayor Koch of (bankrupt) New York was not asked to spend more money in East Brooklyn but to ensure that the garbage was removed from the streets.

The central committee of the organisation goes straight into an evaluation after an action and the organiser plays a questioning and critical role throughout. She asks the difficult questions and insists that the group act democratically. If a leader is not preparing adequately for meetings he or she will be told this in clear terms. If we are fighting a war (and good community organisation is as difficult as a war) it is no good having troops who cannot do the job. If the self interest of community leaders has been correctly identified, namely to build a democratic and broad based (that is, multi-issue) organisation then the leader will respond positively to the criticism. If self interest has not been correctly identified the leader might just as well resign anyway because second class leadership will not do. (There is, however, a great deal of valuing and recognition of the people involved in these organisations). The organisers are supervised by the director of the IAF.

This approach seems to work in three senses. First, about twenty large scale broad based organisations of poor to moderate income people have been built in the USA. They have stayed in existence for over ten years, in some cases, and they continue to grow. Second, they seem to be successful in getting into relationship with major power-holders and bringing about major concrete changes. Third, they do seem to develop people.

These organisations keep away from issues which will divide the community (abortion in Roman Catholic areas for example) and they steer clear of party politics. They also recognise that poor people are conservative, and so they try to take a pragmatic approach about issues which will sustain the organisation. The IAF staff hold the view that it is only possible to build a mass based organisation if issues are selected which most of the members support. Thus, the IAF organisers are wary of people who are committed to one issue, whether housing or education, socialism or feminism, because an over-concentration on one kind of issue will divide and not unify. They are particularly wary of ideologues.

The problems with the approach taken by the IAF have yet to be fully understood. It requires exceptional community organisers. It probably will not result in a national level political movement, which many would see as necessary if large scale social change in favour of disadvantaged people is to be brought about, though by 1990 it was having influence at state and federal level in the USA. However, while the IAF has learned from many of the mistakes made in organising during the 1970s, including its own, I am not sure whether the levels of democracy which its organisations have developed will be sustained when they become even larger and have to undertake research on highly complex issues. Also, the style of the organiser can sometimes be arrogant, and this form of work might be improved by incorporating some of the approaches suggested by Burghardt. But, in my view, the IAF has been far more successful, so far, than anything in Britain, and we have much to learn from its work (see Boyte (1984, 1989) and Jameson (1988) for a more detailed explanation of the principles and practice of broad based organising).

7
Survival

Surviving agency pressure

A student was doing a practical placement with a local authority department which planned to build a community centre in a particular locality. The student spent time liaising with community organisations and eventually formed a group to discuss the plans. At the first meeting some members expressed major reservations and decided to submit alternative plans. But the local authority was not prepared to discuss alternatives and the student found himself being used to sell the existing plan to the residents, that is, getting them to accept a proposal which might not have been in their own interests.

How does a worker cope with this kind of situation? First, it has to be analysed correctly. To some degree all organisations seek to use their employees to control other bodies or individuals with whom an exchange takes place. We need to try to understand, in any situation, how we are being used and whether our work, on the whole, is benefiting the people whose interests we are trying to serve. To analyse this correctly can be difficult. For instance, the student in the example above might well have concluded that the only way the residents were going to get a centre at all was on the terms of the planning department. Consequently he might not have acted very differently, assuming he thought a centre was needed, apart, perhaps, from explaining to the residents what was happening. But at least he would not have been drawn into the process unwittingly.

Once the general situation has been analysed there are usually four options. These are:
(a) conforming to agency expectations;
(b) getting into overt conflict on the issue, and, perhaps, resigning if you lose;

(c)　working clandestinely on matters you consider important;

(d)　accepting the realities of how the agency uses you but working to change them.

I will dismiss simple conformity to agency expectations quickly because, although it is fairly common, this constitutes bad practice. Bear in mind Resnick's dictum (1975, p. 462) that if we do not change the agency we work in, it changes us! As regards the option of getting into a fight with the agency we need to be sure we are strong enough to win. Paradoxically however, the time to make a stand is often at the beginning; then it is easier to state our terms, and we can sometimes earn respect by doing so. But with large authoritarian agencies a worker may still be told to toe the line, and if she persists she may find herself disciplined. She may also be 'on probation' for the first six months which can make self-assertion difficult.

The third option is to work in a clandestine way on matters which one regards as important, to try to avoid being held to account, only to 'play the game' of being supervised, not to keep records, and even to create an outward show of doing what the agency wants. There are occasionally times when one needs to work clandestinely, but there are major disadvantages in making this one's main way of working. First, the worker will not receive support from the agency, so she is bound to feel isolated. In addition she will not be getting the 'critical support' which we all need if we are to develop. Second, she is likely, in the longer run, to be discovered and stopped. Third, if we evade being accountable to the agency for as long as possible this means we have given up the battle to make the agency change, at least from within. Finally, if there are no records or agency backing for our work our successors are most unlikely to take up the same issues, which means that much of the work will have been in vain.

When a worker is at or near the limits set by her employing organisation she needs to build protection. The most common way of doing this is to find someone with power who knows what she is doing and who can defend her if this becomes necessary. Ideally this should be the person to whom she is directly responsible. If a supervisor has approved a worker's action beforehand and that action turns out to have been beyond the limits set by the agency, then she, not the worker, takes the responsibility. For this kind of protection to work it means the opposite of working clandestinely, because the worker must take steps to ensure she has the backing of the people who are protecting her, which means keeping them informed. It may also require a good deal of work to argue the case for the kind of work which the worker thinks should be undertaken.

To conclude, the whole business of creating the space to work in ways we think are appropriate requires careful thought. If, for instance, a worker has made herself highly regarded in the agency by undertaking everything asked of her, her superiors may be prepared to accept, later, that she spends, say 20 per cent of her time in areas of work which are less important to the agency. That, however, is a far cry from wanting to spend 80 per cent of one's time on such work from the first day!

Preserving one's job

I once sat in on a depressing discussion with Richard, a community centre warden who was about to lose his job. His project was funded by the Home Office Urban Aid Programme and the money was due to run out in three months. The education department which administered the project was anxious to transfer it to the social services department, which would have dismissed Richard and used the building for other purposes. The project was tightly controlled by three councillors on the management committee who had little contact with the centre or Richard.

My first thought was that I would rather have had the discussion two years earlier. Three months was too short a time to mobilise support. Ever since the beginning of the project Richard should have been aware that the funding was time-limited. During that time he should have produced information to show what a useful job he was doing. This information would have described some interesting pieces of work and would have used statistics to show, for example, the increase in the numbers of people using the building. He should also have made sure that a flow of this publicity material went unsolicited to councillors, residents' groups, the local MP, the funding organisation and all other interested parties.

Second, Richard should have made strenuous efforts to involve the councillors in the day to day concerns of the centre. Frequent contact with him and with the user groups might have helped those councillors to identify with the needs as he perceived them. Third, he should have made efforts to convert people of influence in the local authority power structure to his cause. He should also have worked on other members of the management committee, besides the three councillors, to convince them of the value of the project. In addition, he might have considered getting strong user-group representatives and possibly sympathetic outsiders onto his management committee. Fourth, he should have prepared outside parties beforehand for the approaching danger. He should have contacted residents' groups, unions, churches, officials from other departments, sympathetic councillors and the Member of Parliament for example. Fifth, he could have asked a sympathetic person to break the story to the local newspaper, which would probably have been pleased to publicise such an item. Finally, having heard unofficially that there was a written proposal to transfer the centre to the social services department, he should have prepared an alternative plan showing how the needs of the area could be better met if his proposal was implemented instead. That way he would have been taking the initiative. His superiors would have had to fight to some degree on his ground, and he would have been building up the two basic elements which are necessary in any effort to change policy; good argument and a broadly based alliance which can bring pressure to bear.

The stresses of the job

If one asks community workers to list the stresses of the job they usually come up with something like the following:

(1) the problem of coping with isolation and the lack of support;

(2)   the frustration of working within a wide range of constraints: limited finance, an employing authority which does not understand and may to some degree be opposed to what one wants to do – linked to this is the frustration of being exposed and not having a cosy bureaucracy to shelter behind;

(3)   the slow progress in work with community groups which often go over the same ground meeting after meeting;

(4)   the weather! If you have no base in the community it is no fun to wait about between meetings in poor weather;

(5)   irregular working hours. This may be an advantage but it can also take its toll on a worker's private life, particularly if she feels she must work long hours, as many workers do;

(6)   the pressure for concrete results;

(7)   the emotional effort of constant innovation rather than routine work, and the strain of constantly having to step back and think carefully about what one is doing;

(8)   the difficulty of having to try to please everyone and of being under many different pressures at the same time.

Workers need to think about ways to relieve this stress. If we do not find productive or functional ways of relieving it our practice is likely to deteriorate because we find ourselves:

(a)   Taking on too much, failing to say 'no';

(b)   failing to choose between priorities, failing to plan, acting purely intuitively, allowing ourselves to be manipulated;

(c)   losing a sense of purpose and a sense of direction;

(d)   burning out;

(e)   getting depressed and physically ill;

(f)   panicking or over-reacting under presssure;

(g)   avoiding difficult situations;

(h)   wasting time by chatting or moaning much of the day.

We need to understand that these are the kinds of stresses we are likely to experience in community work and to find ways of alleviating them.

The need for supervision

It is difficult to survive and to develop our work entirely alone. We often need someone to listen to us, to 'be there' and perhaps to assure us that we are doing a worthwhile job, particularly when there are few concrete achievements to see. This kind of support comes mainly from family or friends. But we also need someone to help us stand back and look critically at our work within a relationship of trust. If this function is carried out well, it can both build up our confidence and ensure that we continue working on ourselves.

But how is that relationship to be achieved? Unfortunately there is no easy answer. Many workers have someone without community work experience as their superior, and the fact that they are also accountable to her may prevent the growth of sufficient trust. Nevertheless this form of supervision can sometimes work well and should be considered, if only because the other options are often not much better in practice.

A model which is often favoured is that of the outside consultant engaged by the agency. This can be excellent, but a consultant is required who is able to empathise not only with the community work task but also with the needs and problems of being an employee within a particular organisation. If outside consultancy does not work it is awful. When arranging such a consultancy a worker should take care to agree the terms of the contract carefully, so that the responsibility is placed on the worker and not the consultant to decide whether the relationship should continue after the first few sessions. Otherwise it is easy to slide into a useless routine which everyone fears to break. The contract also needs to ensure that the consultant serves the worker and not the agency, so that it is clear where her loyalty lies.

The next type of support is that which is provided by contact with other people doing the same work, other community workers, for example. There is no substitute for the support which can be gained from sharing experiences with people who are in the same position as ourselves, and all workers should try to meet regularly with their peers, if there are any around. The problems with this type of group are first, that the potential members may be involved in matters which are so disparate that they have little in common, and second, that the group can become self-indulgent and spend all its time criticising employers. It therefore provides some support but not much self-criticism. Some such groups engage a consultant to help the members look at themselves, and this can work well as long as the consultant knows her job and there is commitment among the members to work at it.

Finally, I found I received a great deal of support from some of the members of the communities in which I worked. My relationship with them was more that of colleague than anything else and just as they used me for support so I used them.

The lesson to be drawn is that no community worker is an island. In an often hostile world the temptation is to withdraw and work on our own. That way we may survive but we do not develop. We need critical support and we must construct a system which can offer that critical support, and which gives us the space to think objectively about our work.

Conscious practice

Although we need other people to help us develop our work, that only accomplishes half the job. Therefore we all need to develop the habit of conscious practice. Much community work is common sense in that if we stop and think carefully about what we are trying to do and evaluate it afterwards we are able to develop into reasonable practitioners. The best way to improve our practice is to try to be as aware as possible of what we are doing and why we are doing it, which can help us identify what needs to be worked on at a particular time.

There are three interlocking areas which we always need to be working at. First, we must identify what knowledge we need in a particular situation. Second, we may lack specific skills. Many skills, however, relate to our personal qualities, which is by far the most difficult area. We may be shy, nervous, dominating, or impatient, which may prevent us performing certain functions well. Most of us are aware of our weaknesses but may be afraid to face them and therefore neglect to work on them. Sometimes we have to learn to live with them. I think I will always be rather inarticulate when caught off guard, but I can compensate for this by preparing for tricky situations beforehand. However, when examining ourselves it is important to look at our strengths too, otherwise our confidence may ebb away completely. We can only face, accept and perhaps overcome our weaknesses if we appreciate our strengths first.

There is also an ethical reason why a critical awareness of our strengths and weaknesses is important in community work. We are to some degree licensed critics. Even if only by implication, we are criticising the status quo when we help people organise to change it. It is the height of arrogance to ignore the beam in one's own eye while drawing attention to motes in other people's eyes.

Developing personal competence

A major area of competence relates to the systematic planning of work, especially new work. I once took over responsibility for organising an examination and I thought I had organised it well. However, the day beforehand the head of department said 'I've ordered the answer books for tomorrow morning'. I realised I had never even considered them! The way to overcome potentially serious problems of this kind when undertaking new areas of work is to write down in advance all the tasks which need to be carried out and to check these with a colleague. Similarly, planning one's work schedule with a prioritised daily list of things to do can be useful. There are of course many aids for this kind of work planning, such as Filofax, but to do it well requires, primarily, appropriate attitudes and self-discipline. The same point applies to developing appropriate filing systems, making mental notes that all incoming letters will be answered within a week, and so on.

Our personal styles also relate in a basic way to how we do our work. Most community workers seek relatively open and informal relationships with those with whom they work. However, we need to take care not to get our private and professional lives too mixed up because different behavioural expectations apply in each. In particular one should try to avoid having intimate relationships with people for whom we have professional or managerial responsibilities.

Many people active in social and community work share one particular Achille's heel – lack of assertiveness. It takes many forms, though a main one is not wanting to do what will displease other people. It also applies to men as much as women. Assertiveness is neither aggression, nor manipulation, nor passivity. It is to do with working out what one feels, thinks or wants in a given situation and communicating this confidently and unambiguously to other people. It links also with communication skills, such as making statements beginnning with 'I, rather than 'you', which are more likely to defuse potential conflict situations. (For example 'When you do X I feel embarrassed'). Another dimension of this is 'saying no'. A close colleague of mine only advises his staff to undertake work which other agencies want them to do if it is good for the worker, good for the agency or makes money! The assertive practitioner is also able to push problems which other people expect her to solve back to those for whom it is a problem. I once agreed to discover information for an inter-departmental working group which I thought was unnecessary, because I was not assertive enough to state that if a particular person wanted that information he should, in my view, find it out himself. Today, I hope I would handle it differently.

There are now many books that can be of assistance to those of us who lack these kinds of skills, for instance, *Staying OK* (Harris and Harris, 1985), *Beyond Fear* (Rowe, 1987), *Your Erroneous Zones* (Dyer, 1977).

The importance of recording

If a worker disciplines herself to write down what she planned to happen, what she did, what actually happened, what she thought about it and what her future plans are, she is performing two functions. First, she is forcing herself to reflect on her actions, to evaluate and, to some degree, to plan ahead. Second, she is making a record of what happened.

All workers should devise a method of recording which suits them, and their agency. One way is to keep a regular diary or log book. Ten lines per night is better than two sides at the weekend, but that too is better than nothing. If you have a good supervisor, the log book can also be an invaluable help during supervision because you will reveal in the written word other points besides those you mention in discussion. The purpose of the log book is largely for training; consequently it is sometimes worth doing a process recording of one meeting you attend. This is a recording which covers chronologically, and in detail, everything that happened, including your thoughts and feelings, as well as non-verbal communication.

The other reason for recording is to do with the needs of the agency. The achievements of community work are by no means self-evident and workers have a responsibility to their agency to show how they are spending their time and what, if anything, they are achieving. Consequently, they should, in my view, provide the agency with summaries of all their work on at least a quarterly basis. When I say summaries, I mean just that since to be of use records must be retrievable. Every so often the record should also contain a review of the stage which the activity has reached and a consideration of the worker's role including, for example, whether she should become more involved or begin withdrawing. This method of recording forces us to think about whether we have our priorities right.

When considering recording community workers are likely to think, principally, of recording only their work with community groups but there are many aspects of our work which are neglected if we restrict our recording to this area. For example, in a project in which I worked we developed a contact-making project which needed careful monitoring. At another stage a major piece of my work was to try to establish better relations with local schools. Ways need to be found of including these kinds of work in one's recording.

Finally, when a worker is preparing to leave her job she must pay attention to bringing her records up to date in order to help her successor decide priorities. She needs to summarise the state she has reached with each piece of work and suggest objectives which he might wish to consider. It can also help to leave one's successor a list of contacts with a few comments on, for example, their position in the community and ways they might help or hinder his work.

8
Afterword

Our ideas about community work relate closely to our often unstated assumptions about the world, which underpin our usually more explicit ideologies and value systems. These in turn influence our beliefs about the role of government, social action and, more specifically, what community work is *for*. To some extent these value systems predispose us to work in certain organisations rather than others, or to adopt particular approaches to our work and to eschew others – thus, they influence our practice.

We then have to reconcile our ideas about how we think the world ought to be with the often harsh realities of how the world is today. While the world is indeed 'socially constructed' it is not easy to break through common perceptions of it and then to 'prefigure' in our practice, a social world operating in markedly different ways. Thus, as community workers, we have to draw upon the range of approaches and skills outlined in this book (and more as well), some of which have been tried and tested, but all of which require continuing critical analysis and constant honing, in such a way that they link positively with our wider vision.

Community work consists, in my view, of a value system and a technology. Simply put, the technology is to do with assisting other people to build, control and manage organisations. The value system has to be, for me, centrally located in a desire to create a better world for people, who, in any given situation, are disadvantaged, and to 'empower' them. Community work is thus, ultimately about social justice, though it is also about democracy.

In the United States those railroad companies which thought their business was railroads went out of business. Those that realised they were in transportation diversified

166

accordingly and survived. It is certain that there will be roles for community workers for the foreseeable future and that the work required of us will mean adapting our technology to changed circumstances. In my view, as long as we hang on to our value system we will be able to undertake our work in such a way as to benefit relatively disadvantaged people in a wide range of settings. Nevertheless, in the future, as now, there will be some situations where we decide not to become involved because a close analysis of the situation leads us to conclude that we cannot use our skills in ways which will benefit the people about whom we are most concerned. Living with and managing the dissonance between our own views about what we think needs to be done and what it is actually possible to do thus requires an ability not to ignore wider political realities, using our technology in a blinkered fashion, but to face them in such a way that we do not lose heart. We each have, ultimately, to find our own answer to this sometimes heart-rending dilemma. If a community worker can get the balance right, and if she can accept the limitations of the work while continually striving to overcome them in order to realise her vision, she is likely to find she has a rewarding, though demanding, job. And she may be surprised how much she can achieve after all, and how much fun she can have doing it!

Further Reading

Alinsky, S. (1972) *Rules for Radicals – A Pragmatic Primer for Realistic Radicals*, New York, Vintage Books. The most refreshing writer on community work I know. If you are likely to become involved in confrontation read Alinsky first, but remember that Britain is not the USA.

Armstrong, J., Hudson, P., Key, M., Whittaker, J. and Whittaker, M. (1976) *Community Work through a Community Newspaper*, London, Community Projects Foundation, 60, Highburg Grove, London N5 2AG.

Association of Community Workers (ACW) (1976) *Knowledge and Skills for Community Work*, London. Short and simple.

ACW (1978) *Towards a Definition of Community Work*, London. A collection of papers relating theory, practice and ideology.

ACW (178) *Conditions of Employment for those Working in the Community*, London. A useful guide on what to watch out for when applying for a job.

ACW (1979) *The Community Workers' Skills Manual*, London. Contains wide range of material in summary form under headings of information, communication and group process.

Astin, B. (1979) 'Linking an information centre to community development', in M. Dungate *et al* (eds) *Collective Action*, London, ACW/Community Projects Foundations, pp. 31–5.

Bailey, N., Lees, R. and Mayo, M. (1980) *Resourcing Communities: Evaluating the experience of six Area Resource Centres*, Polytechnic of Central London.

Baldock, P. (1974) *Community Work and Social Work*, London, Routledge. A good practice theory handbook.

Baldock, P. (April 1982) 'The New Welfare Pluralism' in *Community Development Journal* vol. 17, no. 2, pp. 171–5. A brief and well written critique of the ideas of welfare pluralism.

Baldock, P. (1982) 'Community Work and the Social Service Departments' in G. Craig *et al.*, *Community Work and the State*, London, Routledge. An elegant argument why community workers need to work to organise the client groups of social services departments.

Ball, M. (1988) *Evaluation in the Voluntary Sector*, Forbes Trust. A comprehensive introduction to the various aspects of evaluation.

Barclay, P. (1982) *Social Workers: Their Role and Tasks* (Barclay Report), London, National Institute for Social Work/Bedford Square Press.

Major report on future of social work. Made the case for community social work (with one major dissenting voice).

Barker, H. (Summer 1986) 'Recapturing Sisterhood. A critical look at "process" in feminist organising and community work', *Critical Social Policy* 16, pp. 80–90. A fearless and penetrating examination of how far ideas associated with the Women's Liberation Movement apply or do not apply to community work practice.

Batten, T. R., (1967) *The Non-Directive Approach in Group and Community Work*, Oxford University Press. A series of case studies from the Third World illuminating the idea of the non-directive approach.

Bayley, M., Seyd, R., and Tennant, A. (September 1985) *Neighbourhood Services Project, Dinnington*, Paper no. 12, Department of Sociological Studies, Sheffield University. Draws out the organisational implications for situations where health workers, welfare workers and others attempt collaborative working at neighbourhood level.

Bell, C. and Newby, H. (1971) *Community Studies*, London, Allen & Unwin. An excellent introduction to community studies and different ideas about the nature of community.

Biddle, W. (1965) *The Community Development Process*, New York, Holt, Rinehart & Winston. An early classic community development textbook.

Boyte, H. C. (1984) 'Empowerment' in H. C. Boyte, *Community is Possible*, London, Harper & Row, pp. 125–159. A description of the work in Texas of Citizens Organised for Public Service (COPS) which is one of the newer organisations sponsored by the Industrial Areas Foundation (set up by Saul Alinsky).

Boyte, H. C. (1989) *Commonwealth: A Return to Citizen Politics*, New York, The Free Press.

Bradshaw, J. (1981) 'A taxonomy of social need' in P. Henderson and D. N. Thomas (eds) *Readings in Community Work*, London, Allen & Unwin, pp. 39–42. A widely reproduced article which clearly describes different ways of describing needs.

Brager, G., and Holloway, S. (1978) *Changing Human Service Organizations*, New York, Free Press.

Brager, G. and Specht, H. (1969) *Community Organizing*, Columbia University Press. One of the classic American texts. A bit dated now.

Brenton, M. (1985) *The Voluntary Sector in British Social Services*, London, Longman, 1985. A wide-ranging critique of the idea that voluntary organisations could take over statutory services.

Broady, M., and Hedley, R. (1989) *Working Partnerships: Community Development in Local Authorities*, London, Bedford Square Press.

Bryant, B. and Bryant, R. (1982) *Change and Conflict: A Study of Community Work in Glasgow*, Aberdeen University Press. Case studies and evaluation of some community work practice based, on the whole, on contest tactics. Contains some useful lessons.

Bryant, R. (1979) *The Dampness Monster*, Scottish Council of Social Service, Edinburgh. A short, readable account of a campaign, followed by guidelines on how to organise one yourself.

Burghardt, S. (1982) *The Other Side of Organizing*, Cambridge, Massachusetts, Schenkman. A book arguing that community workers need to develop personal skills.

Clarke, S. (1978) *Working on a Committee*, London, Community Projects Foundation. A useful handbook if you have no experience of committees and even if you have.

Cockburn, C. (1977) *The Local State*, London, Pluto Press. A widely read book arguing that while community work is incorporated by the state, community workers can, nevertheless, make real gains for the working class.

Community Action Magazine, no 41, Jan/Feb 1979.

Community Work Group (1973) *Current Issues in Community Work*, London, Routledge/Calouste Gulbenkian Foundation.

Corina, L. (1977) *Oldham CDP: an Assessment of its Impact and Influence on the Local Authority*, Department of Social Administration and Social Work, University of York. Contains useful material on the main influences on local authorities.

Curno, P. (1979) *Political Issues and Community Work*, London, Routledge. An excellent book with contributions from community workers with varying political perspectives.

Corrigan, P. and Leonard, P. (1978) *Social Work Practice Under Capitalism: A Marxist Approach*, London, Macmillan. Good on analysis. Pretty weak on prescription.

Craig, G. and Derricourt, N., Loney, M. (eds) (1982) *Community Work and the state: Towards a Radical Practice*, Routledge/ACW. Includes a number of thought-provoking articles written mostly from the 'radical' perspective in community work.

Dyer, W. (1977) *Your Erroneous Zones*, London, Sphere Books. Aims to help people get rid of maladaptive behaviour such as guilt and conforming to the expectations of others.

Edwards, K. (July 1984) 'Collective Working in a Small Non-Statutory Organisation'. *MDU Bulletin*, National Council for Voluntary Organisations, London, no. 3/4. A short article indicating some of the problems of collective working.

Francis D. and Henderson, P. *Rural Community Work*, London, Macmillan, forthcoming.

Freire, P. (1978) *Pedagogy of the Oppressed*, Harmondsworth, Penguin. Freire, a Christian Marxist, has developed a technique of 'conscientisation' which he uses mainly in connection with the teaching of literacy in South America. Very interesting, but difficult to read, and repetitive.

Gallagher, A. (1977) 'Women and Community Work' in M. Mayo (ed.), *Women in the Community*, London, Routledge, pp. 121–40. A reflective article containing much practical wisdom. Main content is a discussion of when and under what conditions women and poor people become involved in collective action.

Glampson, A., Scott, T., and Thomas, D. N. (1975) *A Guide to the Assessment of Community Needs and Resources*, London, National Institute for Social Work. A 'must' if you are doing a comprehensive community profile.

Goetschius, G. (1969) *Working with Community Groups*, London, Routledge. A classic book of practice theory in community development.

Hadley, R., and McGrath, M. (eds) (1980) *Going Local*, London, Bedford Square Press, Occasional Paper 1. A useful series of case studies describing social work initiatives based on 'patch' systems of working.

Hadley, R., Cooper, M., Dale, P. and Stacy, G. (1987) *A Community Social Worker's Handbook*, London, Tavistock. A review of the issues involved in putting community social work into practice.

Harris, A. & T. (1985) *Staying OK*, London, Pan Books. The sequel to the best seller *I'm OK You're OK*, which is an introduction to transactional analysis – a simple guide about how to handle life more satisfactorily.

Henderson, P. and Thomas, D. N., (April 1981) 'Federations of Community Groups – The Benefits and Dangers' in *Community Development Journal* vol. 16, no. 2. pp. 98–104.

Henderson, P. and Thomas, D. N. (1987) *Skills in Neighbourhood Work*, London, Allen & Unwin. A comprehensive guide to the practice of neighbourhood community work.

Holloway, C. and Otto, S. (1985) *Getting Organised: A Handbook for non-statutory organisations*, London, Bedford Square Press. A brilliant do it yourself book on organisational development for voluntary organisations. Very practical.

Jameson, N. (ed) (Autumn 1988) 'Organizing for a Change' in *Christian Action Journal*.

Jay, A. (1972) *The Householders' Guide to Community Defence against Bureaucratic Aggression*, London, Jonathan Cape. How to run your campaign against, for example, a motorway, aimed at the middle-class audience. Very good on the psychology of local authorities.

Jones, M. (1984) *Voluntary Organisations and the Media*, London, Bedford Square Press. A useful and readable practical guide.

Key, M., Hudson, P., Armstrong, J. (1976) *Evaluation Theory and Community Work*, London, Community Projects Foundation. A lengthy discussion of the application to community work of the various techniques of evaluation.

Landry, C., Morely, D., Southwood, R., Wright, P. (1985) *What a Way to Run a Railroad: an analysis of radical failure*, London, Comedia. Critical discussion of how far the principles associated with (left) alternative methods of working apply in practice.

Lees, R. and Mayo, M. (1984) *Community Action for Change*, London, Routledge.

Levin, P. (1981) 'Opening up the planning process' in P. Henderson, D. N. Thomas (eds) *Readings in Community Work*. London, Allen & Unwin, pp. 108–14. An interesting article which shows how difficult it is to influence the planning process from outside.

Lloyd, T. and Michaelides, A. (1983) *How to Manage your Money, if you have any*, Community Accountancy Project/Hackney Community Action.

London Voluntary Service Council (1985) *Voluntary but not Amateur: A guide to the law for voluntary organisations and community groups*.

Lowndes, B. (1982) *Making News: Producing a Community Newspaper*, National Federation of Community Organisations.

Lupton, T. and Mitchell, J. D. (1954) 'Neighbourhood and Community', in T. S. Simey and E. Black (eds), *Neighbourhood and Community*, University of Liverpool Press, pp. 15–77. Useful description of how associations developed and how tenants perceived themselves on some Liverpool housing estates.

Mayo, M. (1975) 'Community Development: A Radical Alternative' in R. Bailey and M. Brake (eds) *Radical Social Work*, London, Arnold. pp. 129–43. Argues that the radical potential of community development can only be realised if its repressive aspects are analysed.

Mayo, M. (1979) 'Radical politics and community action', in M. Loney and M. Allen (eds), *The Crisis of the Inner City*, London, Macmillan, pp. 131–48. A relatively sophisticated development of how structuralist (Marxist) ideas might relate to practice.

National Federation of Community Organisations, *Licensing and other Statutory Requirements*.

North Tyneside CDP (1978) *Final Report, Vol. 3, North Shields: Organising for Change in a Working-Class Area*, Newcastle-on-Tyne Polytechnic. Some interesting accounts of attempts to engage in wider campaigns. See especially the section on North Tyneside Housing Campaign.

Ohri, A., Mannng, B., Curno, P. (eds) (1982) *Community Work and Racism*, London, ACW/Routledge.

Payne, M. (1982) *Working in Teams*, London, Macmillan.

Peters, T. J. and Waterman, R. H. (1982) *In Search of Excellence: Lessons from America's Best Run Companies*, New York, Harper & Row. Emphasises the importance of valuing people in management.

Peters, T. J. and Austin, A. (1985) *A Passion for Excellence*, London, Collins.

Pinder, C. *'Community Startup': How to start a Community Group and keep it going* (1985) National Extension College/NFCO. Comprehensive, easy to read. Strongly recommended for community groups.

Piven, F. F. and Cloward, R. A. (1979) *Poor People's Movements: Why they Succeed, How they Fail*, New York, Vintage Books. A classic exposition of the idea that protest only succeeds while militant action continues.

Raynor, P. (1985) *Social Work, Justice and Control*, Oxford, Blackwell. A readable analysis of probation work, which argues that effective practice requires client-centred work based on a contract between probationer, court and officer.

Resnick, H. (1975) 'The professional; pro-active decision-making in the organisation', *Social Work Today*. vol 6, no. 15 (30 October) pp. 462–7. About how to change your organisation rather than letting it change you.

Resnick, H. and Patti, R. J. (1980) *Change from Within: Humanizing Social Welfare Organizations*, Philadelphia, Temple University Press.

Richardson, A. (1983) *Participation*, London, Routledge. A thorough and critical examination of participation in social policy.

Rogers, C. (1961) *On Becoming a Person: A Therapist's View of Psychotherapy*, London, Constable. The main book of one of the founders of counselling, stresses the need to empathise in all successful relationships.

Rote, G. (1979) 'How to cope with the media', *Social Work Today*, vol. 10, no. 22 (30 January). Contains many useful hints.

Rothman, J. (1976) 'Three models of community organisation practice', in F. M. Cox *et al.*, *Strategies of Community Organisation*, Illinois, F. E. Peacock, pp. 22–38. A seminal article expounding three approaches to community organisation: locality development, social action, social planning.

Rowe, D. (1987) *Beyond Fear*, London, Fontana. Aims to help people live and act by acknowledging their own fears.

Salmon, H. (1974) 'Neighbourhood community work in an inner-city neighbourhood' in P. Evens (ed.), *Community Work Theory and Practice*, Oxford, Alistair Shornach.

Shelter, Community Action Team (n.d.) *How to use the Census*, London.

Smiley, C. (Jan. 1982) 'Managing Agreement: The Abilene Paradox' in *Community Development Journal*, vol. 17, no. 1. pp. 54–68. A great story about how not to base what you do on what you think other people's expectations are.

Smith, Jerry (1979) 'An advice centre in a community work project'; in M. Dungate *et al.* (eds), *Collective Action*, London, Association of Community Workers/Community Projects Foundation, pp. 31–5.

Smith, Jim (1979) *Basic Book-keeping for Community Groups*, 2nd edn, London, Voluntary Service Council.

Smith, L. (1981) 'A model for the development of public participation in local authority decision-making' and 'Public participation in Islington – a case study' both in D. Jones, L. Smith, *Deprivation, Participation and Community Action*, ACW/Routledge.

Social Trends, London, Central Statistical Office, HMSO.

Specht, H. (1975) 'Disruptive Tactics' in R.M. Kramer and H. Specht (eds) *Readings in Community Organization Practice* Prentice-Hall, pp. 336–48. A classic article which relates different tactics to collaborative, campaign and contest 'modes' of intervention.

Stanton, A. (1989) *Invitation to Self Management*, Dab Hand Press, 90, Long Drive, Ruislip, Mddx. HA4 0HP. An honest and sympathetic case study of a collectively managed social work agency.

Taylor, M., Kestenbaum, A. and Symons, B. (1976) *Principles and Practice of Community Work in a British Town*, London, Young Volunteer Force Foundation. Useful account of what some workers actually did, including material on umbrella organisations.

Thomas, D. N. (1978) 'Community work, social change and social planning' in P. Curno (ed.) *Political Issues and Community Work*, London, Routledge.

Thomas, D. N. (1976) *Organising for Social Change – a Study in the Theory and Practice of Community Work*, London, Allen & Unwin. A useful basic textbook.

Thomas, D. N. (1978) 'Journey into the actinng community: experiences of learning and change in community groups', in N. McCaughan (ed.) (1978) *Group Work: Learning and Practice*. London, Allen & Unwin.

Thomas, D. N. (1983) *The Making of Community Work*, London, Allen & Unwin. A comprehensive and critical review of community work past and present.

Twelvetrees, A. (1976) *Community Associations and Centres*, Oxford, Pergamon Press.

Twelvetrees, A. (1984) *An Integrated Approach to Community Problem Solving*, School of Social Studies, University College of Swansea, 1984. A detailed case study of my own community development work on a council estate.

Twelvetrees, A. (1985) *Democracy and the Neighbourhood*, NFCO. Mainly about community associations.

Twelvetrees, A. (1989) *Organising for Neighbourhood Development: a Comparative Study of Community Development Corporations and Citizen Power Organisations*, Aldershot, Avebury, 1989. My study of the degree to which community organisations can ensure effective economic development of urban ghettos in the USA.

Waddington, P. (1979) 'Looking Ahead – Community Work into the 1980s', *Community Development Journal*, vol. 14, no. 3. A classic article describing how community work was likely to be incorporated by the State during the 1980s but arguing that there was still scope for effective work.

Waller, B. (August 1986) 'Management by walking about . . . and other good ideas' in *Community Care*, pp. 24–25. Tries to apply some of the ideas of *In Search of Excellence* (Peters and Waterman) to social services departments.

Walton, R. E. (1976) 'Two strategies of social change and their dilemmas' in F. M. Cox, *Strategies of Community Organization*, Illinois, F. E. Peacock *et al.*, A seminal article indicating two very different approaches to the change process.

Willmott, P. (1989) *Community Initiatives: Patterns and Prospects*, Policy Studies Institute, London. A brief but comprehensive summary of a range of community initiatives.

Wilson, D. (1984) *Pressure. The A to Z of Campaigning in Britain*, London, Heinemann. An excellent practical guide. Very readable.

Index

175

self-help guided by community
worker   6–7, 45–7, 61–5,
101–2
self-knowledge, of community
workers   20, 86–7, 148–51,
161–3
self-presentation   19
servicing roles   62–4
sexism   148, 150
Shelter   32, 102, 111
sit-ins   144
size of group   40
Smiley, C.   119
Smith, Jerry   73
Smith, Jim   67
Smith, L.   100
social planning and community
work   6–8, 98–139
social work and community
workers   74–9
socialism   147
Specht, H.   82, 140
'specialist' community
workers   36, 110–14
staff management, by community
workers   70, 124–5, 128–9,
132–4, 133–4
Stanton, A.   49
street representatives   53
stress   158–9
strikes   144
structure, organisational   47–50,
123

Take Care project, Wales   114
Taylor, M. *et al.*   61, 82
teachers   19, 54–5
tenant consultative committees   82
tenants' associations   27, 60, 63–4,
102, 104

Thomas, D.N.   24, 31, 52, 61, 149
tokenism   123
'top down' community work   9–10,
111, 128
town halls   26–7
Twelvetrees, A.   61, 70, 72, 118

unemployment   33, 71–2

viability, assessment of   124
violence, domestic   73–4
voluntary action   80–3
see also community groups
volunteers
management of   79, 129–30
and youth clubs   130

Waddington, P.   105
Wales Council for Voluntary
Action   114
Walton, R.E.   143
Waterman, R.H.   129
welfare pluralism   117–19
Willmott, P.   9, 10, 11, 16, 72
Wilson, D.   145
withdrawal by community
workers   62–5
Women's Aid   32, 111
Women's Liberation
Movement   49, 147, 149–50
women's refuges   103
Women's Royal Voluntary
Service   27
working-men's clubs   27

youth clubs and volunteers   130
youth employment   103, 105
youth workers   54–5, 58